BLOODLINE

HOW TO OVERCOME GENERATIONAL BONDAGE AND REWRITE YOUR FAMILY'S FUTURE

Nalini Tranquim

Ark House Press
arkhousepress.com

© 2025 Nalini Tranquim

All rights reserved. Apart from any fair dealing for the purpose of study, research, criticism, or review, as permitted under the Copyright Act, no part may be reproduced by any process without written permission.

Scripture quotations marked (NLT) are taken from the Holy Bible, New Living Translation, copyright ©1996, 2004, 2015 by Tyndale House Foundation. Used by permission of Tyndale House Publishers, Carol Stream, Illinois 60188. All rights reserved.

Some names and identifying details have been changed to protect the privacy of individuals.

Cataloguing in Publication Data:
Title: Bloodline: *How to Overcome Generational Bondage and Rewrite Your Family's Future*
ISBN: 978-1-7640542-0-1 (pbk)
Subjects: REL012030 RELIGION / Christian Living / Family & Relationships; REL012170 RELIGION / Christian Living / Personal Memoirs; REL077000 RELIGION / Faith;

Design by initiateagency.com

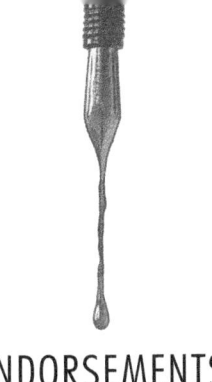

ENDORSEMENTS

"Bloodline" is a powerful testament to the transformative power of Christ's blood in breaking generational curses. The first few chapters had me in tears as I read Nalini Tranquim's honest account of her family's journey through a devastating diagnosis - the same disease that claimed her brother's life. I couldn't help but wonder what I would have done in their shoes and if my own faith would withstand such a challenge. Her story deeply moved me, both challenging my faith and drawing me into deeper trust in God's promises.

What sets this book apart is that Nalini doesn't simply offer inspirational platitudes; she provides a roadmap for believers to actually appropriate the authority we have in Christ. Through her family's story, she demonstrates how we can exchange our natural bloodline—with all its inherited struggles and weaknesses—for the perfect, redemptive bloodline of Jesus.

This book will shake you free from passive acceptance of generational patterns of addiction, illness, and brokenness. It equips you with practical wisdom to stand against the enemy's lies that your future is determined by your past. Nalini's testimony reminds us that when we become children of God, we receive not only forgiveness but a completely new spiritual DNA.

If you've ever felt trapped by family patterns or ancestral struggles, "Bloodline" offers more than hope—it offers freedom through the blood of Jesus Christ. I wholeheartedly recommend this book to anyone seeking to fully embrace their inheritance as sons and daughters of God.

Michelle Deuz
Founder of Prophetic Processing LLC
michelledeuz.com
Prophetic Company Director of Mission Church
imissionchurch.com

When I sat down to read Nalini's book "Bloodline" I was immediately gripped. This is a most inspiring story of love that doesn't let go when situations are declared hopeless. It is raw, passionate, faith inspiring and woven through with Christ's love and the unchanging power of a covenant of blood shed at Calvary. The quest to utterly smash generational curses is a powerful central theme. This book will inspire and help people to face every challenge to their family with unshakeable courage and certainty.

Tim Hall
Founder of Tim Hall International Ministries
timhall.com.au

What a privilege to write an endorsement for Nalini's book "Bloodline." This book is a real page-turner, I could hardly put it down. Nalini's way with words quickly draws the reader into their story, which follows on from her first book, "The Orange Hue." This is a raw and gut-wrenching story which is hard to believe. A story of intense testing, pain, grief, confusion with many twists and turns just to name a few. From tragedy to triumph! Nalini and her husband Sandro are the real deal! Read how they navigated their way through life by God's grace alone. We are privileged to call them dear friends and we heartily endorse this book and everything else that they are doing in life and ministry.

Margaret McCracken
Co-Founder of David McCracken Ministries
davidmccracken.org

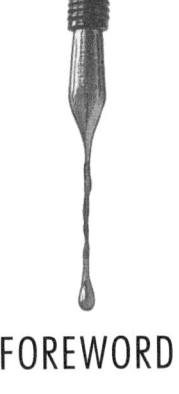

FOREWORD

There are moments in our walk with God when we encounter a truth so profound that it forces us to reexamine everything, we thought we knew about faith. Reading Nalini Tranquim's "Bloodline" has been such an encounter for me.

As I turned each page of this powerful testimony, I found myself simultaneously challenged and comforted. Challenged to confront the areas where my own faith has fallen short and comforted by the unshakable promise that the blood of Jesus is stronger than any generational curse or inherited struggle.

Nalini doesn't write from the safe distance of theological theory. She writes from the crucible of lived experience, where abstract beliefs are tested in the fire of real suffering. When her son faced the same rare disease that had claimed her brother's life, Nalini and her family stood at a crossroads familiar to many believers: Would they accept the narrative of an inescapable "family curse," or would they claim the authority given to them as children of God?

What follows in these pages is not merely inspiration—though you will certainly find that here. Rather, it is a masterclass in applied faith, demonstrating how the promises of Scripture can be activated in our lives even when all earthly evidence suggests otherwise. Nalini shows us, with raw honesty and practical wisdom, how to move from merely believing in Christ's redemptive power to actually appropriating it in our daily battles.

In my years of ministry, I have encountered countless people shackled by the sins and sicknesses of their ancestors, believing themselves powerless against the patterns seemingly encoded in their DNA. "Bloodline" offers a revolutionary truth: when we are born again, we receive a new spiritual bloodline—one that flows directly from the heart of Christ Himself. This divine bloodline carries the authority to break cycles of addiction, illness, broken relationships, and spiritual oppression that have plagued families for generations.

As you journey through these pages, I pray you will do so with an open heart. Allow the Holy Spirit to illuminate areas where you may have unconsciously accepted limitations based on your natural bloodline. Be prepared for uncomfortable revelations - but also for the exhilarating freedom that comes from claiming your true spiritual inheritance.

The book you hold represents more than one family's story. It represents the possibility of a new chapter in your own story - one written not by the failures and frailties of your ancestors, but by the perfect, redeeming blood of Jesus Christ.

May this book be both mirror and map for you: a mirror reflecting the true authority you possess as a child of God, and a map guiding you toward the full expression of that authority in your life and the lives of generations to come.

Michelle Deuz
Founder of Prophetic Processing LLC
michelledeuz.com
Prophetic Company Director of Mission Church
imissionchurch.com

PREFACE

I have come to learn that when we become children of God, we are no longer bound by one's earthly bloodline because we take on the fingerprint, the blood and DNA of Jesus Himself. He doesn't just wash our sins away, He washes *generational* sins and curses away, breaking those sins and curses off our ancestors' lives, our lives and the lives of future generations to come. But if we don't understand the authority available to us in Christ or *how to appropriate that authority in our individual lives*, we become like the fully grown elephant still tethered to the same small wooden stake that held it as a baby, that despite its sheer size as an adult, makes no shred of attempt to break free.

You don't have to settle for smoking, drug or alcohol addiction just because it 'runs in your family'. You don't have to tolerate mental health challenges like depression, anxiety, suicidal tendencies as well as physical sicknesses when you've been told, 'Your grandma had it, your mother had it and therefore you will have it.'

You don't have to carry the addictions of your forefathers that have been passed down for generations. For example, if your dad used to have pornographic magazines stashed under his mattress that you innocently uncovered in your early years, it doesn't mean that you now have to live with the guilt and shame of a pornography addiction. You don't have to accept divorce just because so many marriages in your family-line have ended in divorce. Nor do you have to live bound by the sting of its stigma or speak it over your children's marriages in the future.

And what if sexuality has been an issue in your ancestry? Does it mean that you too are defined by the issues of the past and therefore your future is dictated? No. Not at all.

I am going to take you on a very personal journey and as I unwrap intimate details of my own life, you will begin to see the stitching of the most magnificent love-story come into formation. Holy Spirit will quicken to your heart, elements of your own story. The eyes of your understanding will be opened, and you will be able to walk away equipped with exactly how to break generational sins and curses off your own life, as well as bridge the gap on behalf of your future generations, through the power of Jesus.

CHAPTER 1

THE AFTERMATH

ASHOK RICHARD JALALABADI

When I think back to this moment, it's as if the memory is etched in my mind in real-time, like it's happening right now and not all those years ago. I'm three years old, my dark Indian hair drapes over my ears as if wanting to protect me from what I'm about to hear.

Auntie Bev, my Mama's best friend, was leading me into her lounge room where she sat on the sofa signalling for me to jump up and sit snug upon her lap. Even though I was only three at the time I could still tell by the seriousness of her tone and the lines on her brow, that something was wrong. My mind however was preoccupied because I just wanted to go back outside and play. But when I noticed tears building in her eyes, my fidgeting stopped. She had captured my full attention.

'I have something to tell you.' She started whilst gently stroking my hair back behind my ear. My eyes were fixed firmly on her face as she tried to hold back the tears.

'Your brother has gone to be with Jesus in Heaven.'

Ashok Richard Jalalabadi. I knew he was sick. The last time I had seen him; Mom and Dad had brought him home in a wheelchair. I couldn't recognise his frail figure and Mom had to softly tell me that it was in fact little Ashok. I remember wheeling him around the house and having to be very careful so as not to bump him in any way. Even though he was two years older than me, I felt the need to protect him and take care of him so that he could get better, and we could go back to playing in the garden with wheelbarrows and Chongo Lolos. (A quirky colloquial name for a millipede).

But now he was gone, and he was not coming back.

I learned much later that my reaction to the news was a flinching in my body followed by an immediate squirming off Auntie Bev's lap to run outside and play.

It also became apparent years later that my precious brother had died of a hereditary degenerative blood disorder known as Adrenoleukodystrophy. It was in our family's bloodline and had been passed down for generations.

The person who was closest to me from the time I was born was gone.

In the days, weeks and months that followed, I would often ask my mom where little Ashok was and when he was coming back. She would reply, 'He's gone to heaven to be with Jesus and no, he's not coming back.'

Whilst preparing for the publication of this book, I asked my parents if they would consider penning their own accounts of what those early days looked like for them as a mother and father grieving the loss of their child. Here are their reflections:

Grief That Cannot Be Contained
(From My Mother's Perspective)

"Overwhelming grief consumed us. We cried until there were no more tears, trying to reassure each other—and Nalini—that little Ashok was safe with Jesus, fully healed. Our church family wrapped around us, bringing meals, prayers, visits, and comfort in ways we could never repay. Aunty Bev, as Nalini called her, became a lifeline, caring for her when we were too shattered to function.

But the questions remained. Why did little Ashok have to suffer so much? Why would God allow such pain? And yet, as I sat in the neurologist's office and saw a teenage boy struggling in his wheelchair, his mother exhausted from years of unrelenting care, I felt a strange sense of relief. Perhaps the Lord had spared little Ashok from a lifetime of suffering.

Still, nothing prepared me for the insensitivity of others.

"Well, you're young. You can always have another child."

As if a child could ever be replaced. As if little Ashok's absence could be filled with another name, another face. Others would say, "We know what you're going through," but they had no idea. Only those who have lost a child can understand the depth of this grief.

Some people simply didn't know what to say. At the grocery store, I'd see familiar faces—their eyes would dart away as they quickly turned into another aisle. All I needed was a hug, or a simple word of encouragement. But instead, I'd end up leaving my cart behind, fleeing to the car, where I would sob until I had no more tears left to cry.

The hardest part was trying to restore a sense of normalcy for Nalini. Taking her to playgroup, surrounded by mothers with their little ones, was like reopening the wound again and again. Birthday parties were the worst—because little Ashok should have been there too. I caught myself calling his name when it was time to leave, only to be hit with the crushing reality that he wasn't coming home.

Grief like this wells up from your very bones. You can't control it, and it hits like waves.

Years later, I had to visit a medical specialist. I hadn't realized the office was in the same complex where little Ashok had been diagnosed. The moment I stepped inside, it all came flooding back. I barely made it to the car before I broke down, sobbing into my hands, unable to speak.

Birthdays, Christmases, anniversaries—they never stopped being hard. When the day came that little Ashok would have turned 40, I wept as if we had lost him all over again.

Even now, writing this has been excruciating. But through every painful memory, every tear, we have seen God's sustaining grace. He has carried us. He has given us strength. And though the grief remains, so does the promise that one day, we will see our little Ashok again."

When the Light Went Out
(From My Father's Perspective)

"Looking back over four decades, it still seems impossible to believe that from the moment we first noticed something was wrong in December 1981, to the time our little Ashok went to glory, only four months had passed.

Zimbabwe had just gained independence in 1980, and we had crossed the Zambezi River from Zambia, believing we had stepped into our promised land. Life was new and exciting - my job as a Physics Lecturer in Harare, our home, our church, my newfound faith. I had given my life to Jesus in January 1981, never imagining the trial that lay ahead.

But as the days passed, it was as if the sun slowly retreated behind dark clouds. The clouds thickened, and eventually, all light seemed to vanish. Still, through the darkness, we were never alone. The love, mercy, and grace of our Lord Jesus accompanied us, even when our hearts shattered.

I remember catching the bus to the hospital after work each day, praying desperately for healing. Crying out for a miracle. One evening, as I sat in silence, the Lord spoke clearly that He would answer our prayers, but not in the way we had hoped. A wave of sorrow washed over me as I realized what He was preparing us for.

After the autopsy, we met with the neurologist and saw a teenage boy in a wheelchair—his body frail, his limbs flailing, unable to speak. We realized then, that the Lord in His sovereignty, was sparing us a lifetime of watching our little Ashok suffer. Though our agony was unbearable, tiny slivers of light broke through the darkness. Through our grief, Mary and I clung to each other, drawn closer than ever before.

I struggled to understand why God had chosen to take little Ashok. Why now? Why us? It felt cruel to lose our son when I was still so young in my faith. Yet, in the depths of our sorrow, we were not abandoned. Our church family surrounded us, carrying us through the storm.

Six months later, when one of our church elders lost a child, we went to sit with them. No words were needed. They knew we knew. And in the years that followed, God used our pain to comfort others walking the same road. Even now, there are moments when the memories resurface, sharp and raw. But His grace has been greater still.

The Lord, in ways beyond our understanding, has brought beauty from the ashes. And one day, we will be reunited with our little Ashok in glory. This promise sustains us. Praise God."

As for me, little Nalini, everything changed after the loss of little Ashok Richard Jalalabadi. Immeasurable sadness fell over our home, with long stints of silence framing that first year without him. The joy and laughter in my parents' banter had waned. I so desperately wanted to see them happy again, but a deep loneliness had begun to set like cement within my little heart as the reality of death's finality took root.

THE WARDROBE

From the time I was born, I was emersed in stories by CS Lewis, with 'The Lion, The Witch and The Wardrobe' being my absolute favourite. Mom would curl up with the two of us on the sofa and read stories with such magical expression that you could literally see and touch the scenes before your very eyes.

After the loss of little Ashok, story times subsided as we all retreated into our own grief. Even I, at the tender age of three, was grieving, and I had to figure out how to navigate this loneliness and unshakable sadness that had walked into my little life.

I vividly remember mom picking me up from nursery school, getting home, sliding off the backseat of the car, and scurrying through the front door to deposit my lunchbox on the kitchen sink. I'd then run straight into my bedroom, closing the door behind me. I didn't want to be sucked into the sad silence that now permeated our home. I'd open the door to my oversized "Chronicles of Narnia" wardrobe where the smell of mothballs would hit my nostrils.

As if I didn't want anyone to know where I was, I'd climb into the wardrobe, closing the door ever so gently, then curl up on my own in total darkness, waiting for my eyes to adjust so I could see the outline of the wooden panels above me. I can still smell and feel the old musty wood, even now.

Whilst gazing up, I would begin to talk to Jesus. All I knew was that my big brother was with Him in Heaven because mom had said so, and thinking back now, I guess I must have figured that if I could connect with Jesus, I would still be able to somehow connect with my brother.

Deep down I thought the ceiling would open, just like the back of the wardrobe did in the Chronicles of Narnia story. I was convinced that I would get a glimpse of little Ashok in Heaven.

The ceiling didn't open, but what did happen, is that whenever I asked Jesus what they had been up to that day, I'd see this vivid image in my mind of a bright blue sky, endless fields of yellow flowers, and little Ashok running through them with all the other children around him. Jesus was with them. It was almost like He was their babysitter. They were all smiling, giggling, chatting, running around and playing, before the image would be interrupted with the distant sound of my mom's voice calling me to dinner.

As I stepped out of the wardrobe, I'd be surprised at how the light in the room had dimmed from the time I had gotten in. The sun was setting, and time had obviously passed, its warm and gentle light reflecting on my bedroom walls, with shadows of swaying branches and rustling leaves that somehow brought comfort to the grieving heart of a lonely, little, and hungry girl.

After dinner, dad would send me to brush my teeth and then I'd get tucked into bed. I'd lay awake, straining to hear mom express her concern to dad at the amount of time I spent in the wardrobe.

'It's literally everyday Ashok,' she'd say.

I'd hear the clanging of coat hangers as dad prepared his suit for work the next day.

'Well, it's obviously her thing,' dad would reply a few moments later.

The gap between their grieving words was too long for this little one to remain present. I'd nod off and before long, the early morning sounds and smells of Africa would begin to awaken the senses. A new day reflecting on the walls with new shadows bouncing. The smell of smoke emanating from the worker's quarters filled the air as they prepared food for their children, whilst the hoopoe bird sat on the fence singing its song.

But little Ashok's bedroom was still empty.

Days rolled into weeks, and weeks into months. The wardrobe became my safe space, and it is where my conversations with the God of the Universe first began. Little did I know that the longing of my heart to be with my big brother is what brought me to Jesus.

My parents didn't know what was going on in the wardrobe, but I remember mom trying to figure out ways to draw me out. She arranged play dates and even signed me up to some kid's program at the local church on Friday afternoons. Then out of nowhere, I announced that I wanted to learn how to play the piano. I am so thankful that my parents really listened to me and did everything they could to make this unexpected desire happen. It's ultimately what drew me out of the wardrobe and led me even closer to Jesus.

A year passed when I heard Evangelist Billy Graham speak on television of the very same Jesus that I talked to every day in the safety confines of my wardrobe. Yes, the wardrobe was still a daily ritual for me at this point.

It was only after hearing Evangelist Billy Graham and watching his pianist play the old hymn 'Just As I Am,' when I suddenly knew, as I described in my book 'The Orange Hue',

> *"I didn't just want to play the piano, sing, and put a smile on people's faces – I wanted to introduce people to the love of Jesus through music."*

This was now longer about music. It was about Jesus and introducing people to Him and His perfect love.

If you haven't read 'The Orange Hue,' I encourage you to do so as it will frame the back story and provide greater context to what is about to unfold in the coming pages.

Scan code for The Orange Hue. *Available in paperback, eBook and audio book format.*

THRESHOLD OF A DREAM

My book 'The Orange Hue' ended with Sandro and I walking along the pier in Geraldton, Western Australia. We had just arrived home a few days prior, following a whirlwind album production trip to the USA and UK, and now I was right in the throes of post-production for the upcoming album Today | Tomorrow. Sandro's business was taking off, and the boys were settled back in school. I had finally accepted that this is where God wanted us and had started the ball rolling in looking for a home for us to call our own.

I resumed classes with my music students, and was right back in the shed studio, preparing for the launch of my first full length album.

Memories of me curled up in my wardrobe after my brother had passed came flooding back in my mind. Hours of chatting to Jesus and imagining what little Ashok was up to in Heaven, and Mom and dad so desperately wanting to draw me out of my grief. Those early days of piano lessons, and practicing my songs in front of my teddies, and then performing in front of my audience of two, mom and dad. Oh, just to see them smile again made it even more worthwhile.

Fast forward to Billy Graham unlocking in my heart a desire to introduce people to the love of Jesus through songs and stories, and all the hurdles faced along the way. I had thought becoming a worship director in London was the ultimate call on my life but, when I found myself on the shores of Western Australia, broken and disgruntled, I had no concept of what was ahead.

I never would have imagined that just six years later I would have a full album within my grasp, and one that I would be able to share with the world. Here I was, standing on the threshold of a dream come true.

There was so much to plan and prepare for. Continual back and forth with our producers in Nashville, as they made tweaks to the tracks and then would send them back for us to review. We as a family would listen to the songs in the car, on our phones, and any other speakers we had lying around. It was exhilarating and all consuming.

I had to map out what the album release party would look like. I needed a venue, and volunteers to help with ushering in guests, album sales and the overall running of the event. It was a lot to comprehend, but I was ready. I had been preparing my whole life for this moment. This was the beginning, and I couldn't contain the excitement within my heart.

CLASS CAMP

As I gazed out of the window finishing off the last few dishes in the sink, I noticed our youngest son Björn walking home from school. He didn't look okay. He was darker than usual, which I put down to way too much time in the sun without a hat. But today he looked drawn and fatigued and was dragging his feet.

It was almost the end of third term, and school holidays were just around the corner. We all needed a break as it had been a big year. Ramon our eldest son, was in his second last year of high school and Björn, his first. I knew that Björn was particularly exhausted as he adjusted to the new pressures of growing up. Ramon had already gotten in from school and was in the games room tinkering on his guitar.

I dried my hands and dialled the number to our doctor's surgery to book Björn an appointment. He hadn't been looking his usual chirpy self since getting back from the USA, just three months earlier. And when I thought about it, there were even a few days during the album recording in Nashville where he was just too exhausted to do anything. The niggle in my heart had been growing for some time now, and so it was good to know that an appointment was locked in for when he got back from school camp.

Björn was so excited to be going away with his classmates and favourite teacher Mrs Keys. I was glad it was Friday, as he needed the weekend to rest up, before the long road trip up north. We all spent Saturday shopping and preparing the items on his camp list, and first thing Monday morning, we stood alongside the other parents as we waved our kids goodbye, secretly jumping up and down at the prospect of a week's respite.

About halfway into that week, I received a text message from Mrs Keys to say that Björn just wasn't himself. She first noticed it whilst on a hike with all the other children earlier in the day. She was leading the charge whilst everyone followed, when some of the kids started calling her name. When she turned around, she noticed that the children had stopped walking. As her gaze adjusted, she saw Björn right at the back of the line, sitting in the dirt too tired to keep going. She hastily made her way past the concerned faces of the other children and knelt down beside him to check on him. She felt his temperature and gave him a sip of water, asked a few questions, and then helped him back up.

We texted back and forth with the usual checks and ticks, 'Did he have any breakfast? Has he been drinking enough water?' And of course, the inevitable, 'Has he been wearing his hat?' The sun of Western Australia is brutal in the shade at the best of times. She reassured me that she would keep an eye on him for the rest of the trip and for me not to worry.

I continued with my music students whilst also working on the album, and liaising with the catering company and venue, as we prepared for the upcoming album launch. We also had a series of house concerts lined up, where we had planned evenings in our home with food and fellowship, followed by storytelling intertwined with some of the new songs on the album, so as to give people a taste of what was to come.

It was a very busy time for my husband Sandro in his business, but we still managed to squeeze in sporadic house viewings as we were committed to settling down and making Geraldton our home. Ramon was pushing to finish the term strong, and it was all systems go, and I was counting down the days to Björn coming home. He remained constantly in the back of my mind as the niggle in my heart continued to grow.

UPENDED

It was Friday and the last day of term. Ramon had left for school while Sandro and I headed out to see a property that ticked all the boxes on paper. When we pulled up outside, my heart skipped a beat. It was exactly what we had been dreaming of. It even had a granny cottage that would be absolutely perfect for my folks. We didn't hesitate. We put in our offer straight away and set up a second viewing for later the following week because we just knew this was the house we had been looking for. Finally, we were going to have our forever home. We had travelled and moved around so many times in the previous sixteen years, so the thought of moving in once and for all, and putting our roots down, was a dream come true.

I'd finally have my recording studio sitting snug amongst the trees where I could breathe in inspiration, write, compose and create content to my heart's content! (Excuse the play on words here).

Sandro would have his own shed where he could tinker till the cows come home, and the boys would literally have enough space to get lost in.

My parents would be looked after, and I'd be able to pop into their place for a cuppa and a chinwag whenever needed.

I was on cloud nine for the rest of the day and I couldn't wait for Björn to get home, so that we could all have dinner together and announce to the boys that our offer had been accepted.

As soon as Björn walked in the door, I was horrified at how sun burned and dehydrated he looked. It even seemed like he had lost weight. He complained of a bit of a headache, and said he just wanted to lie down. I told him he needed to eat something first, and so while he jumped into the shower, I rustled up something scrumptious. I knew our plans to announce the house wasn't going to happen that night as my boy needed some sleep. And sleep he did. In fact, he hardly moved between his bed and the sofa all weekend. I kept a close eye on him between batches of laundry, meal prep, checking on folks, Ramon's mates popping in and out throughout the weekend, and making cups of tea for Sandro who was building yet another vehicle in the shed. Weekends were always a much-needed breather, and an opportunity to tinker and just be. No studio time, no students, just family.

Come Monday, Björn looked just as exhausted and dehydrated as he did when he walked in the door on Friday. He hadn't eaten much throughout the weekend apart, from salt and vinegar crisps and jalapenos. Not an odd combination for him, as he always had a thing for salt and heat. I was relieved that he had a doctor's appointment booked, as we really did need to get to the bottom of what was going on.

I was still in the middle of reviewing the "Today | Tomorrow" album tracks and spent most of the day working in the studio, whilst checking up on Björn now and then to see how he was doing. He was curled up on the sofa watching "Ratatouille" again. By Tuesday, there was not much change.

It was already Wednesday morning, and I was up at the crack of dawn, in my studio with my headphones on, when my mobile rang. It was Sandro from inside the house. I felt a cold chill creep up my spine, as why on earth would he be calling me? I slowly answered and could tell that something was wrong. 'Babe, Björn has just been throwing up.'

My mind raced back over the last few days to the time he'd gotten home from his class camp. He hadn't eaten enough to justify throwing-up, so I knew this was serious and that we had to act fast and get him to the emergency department immediately.

By the time we arrived at emergency, Sandro had to carry Björn's limp frame in his arms. The smell of hospital detergent hit my nostrils with the same speed as our pace. My heart was racing, my mind recollecting the last few weeks as I yelled out, 'Can someone PLEASE help?!'

Right at the other end of the corridor I noticed our dear friend, Dr Apaks Dede staring back at us. He was a Paediatrician at the hospital and must have heard my heart wrenching cry, so immediately came running. There was a mad scramble by a swarm of doctors and nurses as they directed my fear-stricken Sandro to a bed where he promptly lay our boy down.

Björn's veins had collapsed by this point, as the team struggled to get a line into his arm. Everything was a blur. I could vaguely hear Dr Dede giving orders as his sturdy frame leant over my boy. His commanding presence comforted me. All we could do was stand and stare, while I quietly whispered, 'God, help my son.'

We didn't know till much later, that our boy had been put on a critical watch list throughout the night. Apparently those twelve hours were make or break. I'm so grateful that I didn't know this at the time, but the medical team honestly didn't think he would make it through the night.

It was already the early hours of Thursday morning when one of the Doctors on duty came through and suggested that we go home and catch up on a few hours' sleep. They assured us that they would call us immediately if anything changed.

Wearily we dragged ourselves home to bed, crashed, and woke to the sound of our alarm. I'd had my first in a series of House Concerts booked for that night. Chairs and crockery had arrived while we were at the hospital the day before. I was obviously going to have to cancel everything, but my brain was spinning, and my heart was churning.

We then remembered that we had our second house viewing booked in for that same morning. Sandro felt it was important for us to still attend, because we were right in the throes of an offer that had been accepted. He assured me that we wouldn't stay long so that we could make our way back to the hospital straight after.

PAUSE AND PONDER

Has there ever been a time in your life when you thought you were heading down one path, and suddenly out of nowhere, everything changes, throwing every plan into disarray? As you continue to read through the pages that follow, I encourage you to jot down any scenes from your own life that bubble to the surface. As you jot down those scenes, remind yourself of the thoughts and feelings that followed. As you do, I believe Papa God will use this to prepare your heart for a deep work of healing and restoration, that will not only impact you personally, but the lives of your loved ones also.

CHAPTER 2

THE GROUND WAS GONE

CONFLICTED

The house was even more perfect that day than it had been a week ago. I knew the minute we stepped into the hallway that it would be an oasis for us. Maybe considering what had happened yesterday, I was feeling an even stronger tug for a safe space to come home to, where we could rest and recoup.

The wooden beams reminded me of the Tudor house I grew up in as a little girl in Zimbabwe. The country style kitchen overlooking the veggie garden, and the granny cottage just beyond, was a dream come true. The palm trees overlooking the swimming pool reminded me of the palm tree I saw in my mind's eye before leaving London six years prior. This house was exactly what my heart had longed for.

Then the stark reality of my boy in hospital hit me. We had to go. I needed to be by his side. We finished up and I buckled my seatbelt whilst the agent discussed with Sandro what else was needed from our side to proceed with the purchase. We had come in two separate vehicles as Sandro needed to visit a client site before joining me at the hospital.

By the time I arrived back at the hospital, Björn's best friend Tom had popped in to visit. He was sitting on the edge of Björn's bed. I grabbed a photo of the two of them together just as the Paediatrician on-call walked in. He pulled me aside to have a private word.

'We need to get your son to a specialist hospital in Perth as soon as possible.' he said. I told him that Sandro usually finished work around five and that we could easily hit the road soon after that, which would get us into Perth around ten o'clock that night. I suddenly remembered that I still needed to cancel that night's event.

He looked at me with confusion. 'I don't think you understand,' he started slowly. 'Your son is in a critical condition. We have a helicopter waiting and you have thirty minutes to grab a change of clothes.'

I must have responded with a completely blank stare, because it was the words that followed, that shot me into action.

'If we delay, your son might not be here by ten tonight.'

I hastily walked back into the ward, dialling Sandro's number. I sat at Björn's bedside, placing my hand in his. His frailty hit me as I waited for Sandro to pick up. My mind was spinning. Ramon and my parents were at home waiting for news. How could any of this be happening? Sandro eventually answered and I put him on speaker. I explained that Björn needed to be flown to Perth straight away and that we literally have minutes to figure this out. Björn and Tom sat quietly as they listened.

I asked Sandro if he could bring us a quick change of clothes and went on to say that I would be cancelling the house concert straight after this call. Out of nowhere Björn profusely interrupts and says, 'You are *not* cancelling the concert, Mom. You have waited years for this moment.' Tears welled up in my eyes. I could feel a lump in my throat as I sat conflicted.

There was a pause. No one spoke. For someone on the outside looking in on this conversation, it would have looked as though we were *all* in shock. I guess we were. Nothing made sense, everything had happened so quickly. There was an air of urgency. I hadn't even had a chance to ask the Doctor what was going on, and now I've got this house concert thrown into the mix and my son telling me that I still must do it.

The pause broke when Sandro, on the other end of the phone, said, 'I agree with him babe. I'll go with Björn. Ramon and your parents can support you tonight, and then you drive down to Perth tomorrow.'

I never envisioned that I would be in a state of conflict for my first ever house concert. Sandro and Björn were in the helicopter within the hour, while Ramon, my parents and I prepared to welcome Pastors and Community Leaders into our home. My heart was broken. I was scared, I felt alone in my thoughts, and I had no idea what was ahead.

Have you ever been in that place? Where you feel as though you are the only one on the entire planet going through what you are facing? It certainly felt like that to me. I didn't even know how I was going to make it through the next few hours.

THE CONCERT

My tummy was churning. I hadn't hosted an event like this before. My husband wasn't with me, and worst of all my youngest boy was in hospital over four hundred kilometres away, fighting for his life.

Pastors and Community Leaders began to arrive. Ramon and my parents helped to welcome our guests and made them feel right at home. No one even noticed that Sandro and Björn were not there. I was relieved actually. I knew if I had to mention it, I would only end up in tears.

Trays of food and drink were being passed out and the sound of content conversations echoed throughout my home. I slipped out to the bathroom for a moment to catch my breath. I could see agony in my eyes staring back at me in the mirror. My palms were sweating, the butterflies were churning, I could feel a headache coming on. 'Oh God, help me.' I cried. I took a deep breath, put a smile on my face and headed back into the lounge room, calling my guests to find their seats.

There was pin drop silence as everyone waited with bated breath for me to start. I had to force my thoughts back into the room as I was already in Perth desperate to find out what was going on with my boy. My fingers began to stroke the keys, just as I had done countless times before. The melody washed over my very own heart as I began to share stories and sing. This was something I had longed to do from the time I was a little girl.

There were moments of laughter, tears, deep contemplation and then, as the evening ended, I found myself asking the audience if they had noticed that neither Sandro nor Björn were present. A murmuring buzz broke out as our guests looked around the room and came to the realisation that they were in fact missing. As I shared the story of what had happened just yesterday, the buzz died down to a deadly hush. And then I began to softly play the introduction to 'Stripes'. A song on my "Today | Tomorrow" album that I have sung many a time since its release.

Stripes

In that place of weariness,
I look to You for strength.
Lest I lose my effectiveness,
I surrender to You the reins.

Standing now with open arms

Upheld by Your Right Hand.
Lifting my head toward heaven.

Let Your glory shine,
Let Your healing,
Divine healing
Arise.

Let there be healing through music,
Won't You pour out Your Spirit,
Flood my soul.

Scan code for the original version of Stripes:

 The glory of God came down. I could feel His presence. The whole room was saturated in a sense of awe and wonder. Ladies and gentlemen were crying. Some had their hands raised, others were on their knees weeping before Him. I could see that God was touching every single heart present. This moment had nothing to do with what I had just shared. This was a one-on-one encounter with our Lord and King. He was meeting every single person at the point of their own individual need. I couldn't believe what my eyes were witnessing. God was pouring out His presence on our Pastors and Community Leaders in such a tangible and magnificent way.

As I locked up the house and whilst putting off the lights, my Ramon came through and placed his hand on my back. 'You did good Mom, you did good.' He knew tonight would have been a battle for me. Yet in this very moment as I pulled him close and gave him a big squeeze, there was a peace emanating from my mama's heart. Instead of sitting at my son's bedside tonight, I was positioned in worship before my God. There is no better starting line when walking into the trials of life from time spent at the feet of Jesus in worship. You might not know what tomorrow holds, but you have a God in heaven who does.

THE BOARD ROOM

I slipped into Ramon's room and kissed him goodbye. He was on school holidays for the week and had plans to catch up with his mates. My parents were right there if he needed anything. He gave me a hug and I promised to keep him up to date.

It was still dark when I left the house for the four-hour drive to Perth, but I didn't mind it. I needed this time to pray and worship on my own. What I didn't know at the time was the Lord was using these few hours to prepare my heart for what was ahead.

By the time I arrived at the hospital in Perth, Björn was settled into a ward and had a drip. He was looking bright considering and was happy to see me. Sandro was by his side, and they were both keen to hear how last night's event had gone.

What followed was a week of extensive tests and it was gruelling. Everyday brought with it the desperate need for answers, and every night Sandro and I would return back to the hospital accommodation with our questions still unanswered.

It was evident that our Björn was not okay and the concern on the brows of the Doctors didn't help settle our hearts in any way. Sandro and I tried to remain positive in the wait. In between tests and scans, we would curl up with Björn on his bed, to chat, watch cooking shows and listen to track updates as and when the producer sent them through. We'd ring Ramon and my parents to say hi and would tell them to just keep praying.

Eventually after a week of waiting, Sandro and I were called into a Board Room to run through the results of his MRI. I knew it couldn't be good if they needed a whole Board Room to reveal the results. I could feel my heartbeat escalating as we walked down the hospital corridor that stank of bleach.

As we stepped into the Board Room, I suddenly became overwhelmed at the number of medical staff sitting around the table. There must have been at least eight Doctors present, all of whom were staring back in silence at this unsuspecting couple who had no idea what they were about to discover. Sandro pulled out a chair for me to sit when my eyes caught sight of multiple television screens that were mounted on the walls and scattered across the room. On them were images of my son's brain from his recent MRI.

I froze.

I felt this rush of anxiety cursing through my veins. It was as if time stood still. There was pin drop silence in the room as I felt the stares of Sandro and the doctors around me. My body temperature plummeted, and my lips began to quiver as I attempted to exert whatever trace of courage I had to blurt out, 'This is what killed my brother.'

No one moved.

With my eyes still fixed to the images in front of me, my mind reversed back into time to those early conversations with my mama after my brother had passed away. 'Mom, why did little Ashok die?' I'd sporadically ask from time to time. 'The Doctors didn't really know Poppy,' she would respond with the exact same gentleness and compassion she always had whenever I raised the question. 'All they knew when they did his autopsy, was he had shadows on his brain.'

As if being sucked into a vortex, I suddenly found myself back in the Board Room, surrounded by the mute and shocked faces of doctors. I stood frozen in front of those intimidating televisions screens with my Björn's MRI plastered all over them.

There they were. Shadows on his brain.

I can only describe what followed as a frenzied panic like a pool of piranhas feasting on their prey as the doctors with raised voices debated this game changing revelation that had just been dropped into their laps.

Whilst all the commotion took place, Sandro signalled for me to come and join him at the table. Suddenly my legs felt like jelly, as if I'd just run a marathon. I needed to sit down, and I needed to catch my breath. As I did, I closed my eyes trying to drown out the voices and shot up a prayer to heaven, 'Oh God, give us strength.'

It was about three days later when Björn's Neurologist sat Sandro and I down in a private room and broke the devesting news.

'Your son has what's called "Adrenoleukodystrophy". It is a very rare hereditary degenerative blood disorder that has no cure and no survival rate. Your son has days, possibly months, and best-case scenario, he may even have a few years to live,' And as if that wasn't enough to digest, he went on to say, 'But he won't live past his eighteenth birthday.'

I felt as though I had just been stabbed in the chest, multiple times. I suddenly became aware at the strength of my grip on Sandro's hand. As I let go, I looked into Sandro's eyes for some sort of comfort. It seemed that he was looking into mine for the same.

My mind raced back over the last fourteen years, from the time since Björn was born. He was so full of energy. He was a feisty little so and so, (obviously took after his dad) with a sharp-witted sense of humour. He loved anything and everything to do with adrenaline. (Or should I say, the disbursing thereof). Surfing, sand dunning, motor bike riding, martial arts, the lot. He would drive us all up the wall, but oh what I would give to take this illness from him.

We didn't say anything to Björn when we kissed him goodnight that night. Sandro and I hardly said a word to each other as we walked down the hospital corridor, took the lift and headed back to our accommodation that night.

We'd hardly gotten in the door when Sandro said he needed to take a shower. I didn't know what to do with myself and so I walked into the bedroom, lay on the bed in a foetal position and cried. It felt like the ground beneath my feet was gone. I called my dad and shared the news with him. He quietly listened. In utter exhaustion, I finished with, 'Dad, I don't have any assurance for tomorrow,' to which he so gently yet firmly replied, 'Poppy, your only assurance is Jesus.'

I could hear the shower in the background. I envisioned the water running down Sandro's back in the same way the tears ran down my face. My phone pinged. It was a text message from my sister in Botswana. It was six simple words. 'Find solace in your music sis.'

She didn't even know about the meeting we had just walked out of, nor the starkness of reality that we were walking into. I sifted through the tracks that we were almost done finalising and played 'Stripes' as I cried myself to sleep.

PACING

The following morning, I woke to Sandro patting me on my shoulder. 'Babe.' he said, with an urgency in his tone as he placed a cup of tea on the bedside table. Immediately my thoughts recollected the previous day's events. I felt sick in the pit of my stomach as I propped the pillows up behind me. If only it was just a terrible dream.

'Babe,' he said again, as if he knew to interrupt my brain that was already running a million miles an hour. I took a sip of tea and then looked at my man. 'I had a dream last night,' he said. He seemed to be in shock. 'Oh?' I asked half excitedly. My eyes were still puffy from the night before. I waited a few seconds for him to continue. It was as if he was revisiting the scene.

'I saw Jesus on the cross,' he blurted out. He paused. I knew there was a depth to this dream and so I didn't dare move.

'As I looked closer, I saw Björn in a hospital bed beside him.' This was not a normal dream for Sandro. Suddenly I had goosebumps shooting up and down my body. I knew this was a message from God for us.

'Then what did you see?' I asked.

'There was an IV line coming from Jesus' side straight into Björn.' Immediately I saw the image in my mind's eye. The tears began to roll down my cheeks as I quietly sang an old hymn that I used to sing as a little girl.

> 'O the blood of Jesus.
> O the blood of Jesus.
> O the blood of Jesus,
> It washes white as snow.'

From that moment onwards, we kept that image in our hearts.

The days that followed consisted of regular visits back and forth to Perth for continual testing. My darling parents had to go through the painstaking process of writing out a detailed report of exactly what had happened in the days leading up to their precious son's death.

Björn was not well enough to return to school, but we tried to keep things as normal as possible at home as we still had Ramon to consider. Ramon was in his final term of year eleven. He had just one more year to go and he would be done with school. We were so proud of him. He had taken off in drama and music, and we were excited for what was ahead of him.

Our church community and friends from across the world rallied around us. There was a constant flow of people popping in to see Björn, meals being dropped off, text messages with prayers and words of encouragement, that kept us going throughout the day to day.

The album was near completion, but it really seemed so trivial in comparison to what we were facing. We still had a date locked in for the album launch party, which was only a few weeks away, and I certainly wrestled with whether to continue ahead with it or not. I wasn't sure, so remained in the wait and see mode.

Sandro and I found ourselves back in Perth with both Ramon and Björn this time. We all needed to be tested to see if any of us were a blood match to help Björn with a possible Bone Marrow Transplant.

Every day was a ticking time bomb for him, and we were all aware of the urgency for Björn to start treatment. At this stage and after much prayer and deliberation, it looked as if Björn and I would have to move to Perth, and that if we did go the route of a Bone Marrow Transplant, it could take anything between nine months to two years.

Sandro would have to remain in Geraldton to continue with work so we could pay the bills, and Ramon would stay with him to continue with school. I hated the thought of this. But I also knew that we would do whatever was needed for our boy's health.

We'd just had a whole day of tests and more tests. We got back to the hospital apartment that night, grabbed a bite to eat and crashed. The following morning, I woke up completely spent. My tests were done but Sandro, Ramon and Björn still had further tests that needed doing.

I asked Sandro if I could stay back as I just couldn't face being at the hospital again, and I needed some time out, on my own. He agreed and the minute I closed the door behind them, I felt this avalanche of emotion well up from within my gut.

Without delay, I was on my knees, weeping before the Lord as I began travailing in the Spirit. It literally felt like I was in labour. I knew I was bridging the gap through deep intercession for my boy.

Before long I began pacing up and down, beseeching God for a solution. I just couldn't see how we as a family would cope with separating during such a critical time like this. We needed to be together.

The medical team had made it very clear that while a Bone Marrow Transplant was the only possible way forward at this point, every step of the process was a risk that could result in the loss of Björn's life. How was I as a mother, meant to face a potential outcome like that, *alone*, with my husband and eldest son four hundred kilometres away?

'Father God, there *has* to be another solution.' I cried out, repeatedly. My eyes were bloodshot, my body ached from travailing. The pacing slowed and I could feel exhaustion setting in when my phone rang.

It was the lead doctor from Björn's metabolic team. She asked if now was a good time to talk. I wasn't sure if I was ready for any more bad news, but I politely agreed that now was as good a time as any. I held my breath.

She went on to say that Björn's case had come up in conversations with a Neurologist based in Adelaide, South Australia. He was on the Board of Directors for a clinical trial in stem cell transplanting that was taking place in Boston, USA. I couldn't understand why she was telling me all of this. But it was what she said next that made my heart flutter.

The doctor explained that as she described Björn's symptoms in more detail, the Neurologist felt strongly that Björn may qualify and if he did, he could be offered the chance of a stem cell transplant. It was a much more advanced and safer option than bone marrow transplant. My head was spinning as I took in what she was saying. She asked if I would like to speak to Sandro to see whether we would be interested in commencing the testing process for this.

I didn't have to think about it, and I didn't have to run it by Sandro. I *knew* without a shadow of a doubt that this was my Heavenly Father answering my prayers. 'We are absolutely interested.' I said without hesitation.

The doctor advised that she'd get the ball rolling straight away, and that if Björn was accepted, we would have to relocate to Boston for the treatment. I hadn't expected that last part, but as unexpected as it was, I still knew my God was all over this and we would do whatever was necessary.

ALBUM FAREWELL

After a couple of weeks of demanding tests, we got the call from the USA to say that Björn had been accepted into the clinical trial, and that we needed to pack our bags and get ready to leave. They advised that time was of the essence, and that they would notify us immediately when a place became available. They knew Björn had a window of opportunity before his health would deteriorate and he wouldn't be strong enough to cope with the treatment. We packed our lives into a shipping container on a friend's farm and waited for the call.

Some dear friends of ours asked what our plans were for Ramon. He was getting ready to commence his final year of high school, but at the same time, we were a family in crisis. They challenged us to allow Ramon to stay in Australia and for Sandro and I to go to the USA with Björn alone. We couldn't bring ourselves to do this.

It was hard enough contemplating a family separation for the Bone Marrow Transplant in Perth, let alone being separated by thousands of miles between us. I also knew that I would struggle to forgive myself if Björn did die during his treatment and the boys didn't have an opportunity to say goodbye to each other. No. We were going to face this together no matter what.

What had been months of preparation for an album launch, turned into an album farewell. The whole community had been rocked by Björn's diagnosis, and while I thought the evening was designed to be the start of taking my stories and music across the globe, it appropriately became a celebration of a young boy's life, and ultimately, an evening for the community to gather and say goodbye.

What I learned from this whole experience is that sometimes we formulate in our mind's eye just how the future is going to look. I quit my job, took a year out to hone in on my craft, write the album and then jumped on a plane to the USA to get it recorded. Now I was ready for this lifetime dream of mine to eventuate. We were going to launch the album and then take it on the road and share the love of Jesus. Instead, the inevitable curveball hit, and suddenly life was nothing like what we had planned for it to be.

This whole scene seems to be a repeat of the eighteen-year-old girl we encounter in my book 'The Orange Hue,' who had jumped on a plane from Zimbabwe to England to pursue her musical dream, only to discover a few months later that she was pregnant with her boyfriend's baby.

Is this how life works? Do we just jump from one hurdle to the next, to the next, with no reprieve? Is there the fulfilling of dreams or are we just bound by whatever life throws at us, where we simply continue wading through disappointment after disappointment?

Right then, I honestly didn't care, and I didn't have the bandwidth to figure it out either. I just wanted my boy to be okay, and my family to be together.

The most poignant moment of the album release party was towards the end of the evening when I looked out across the five hundred guests in the room. I turned to Björn who was sitting right on the front row with his teachers and thirty classmates. His eyes were glued to mine. I could see how proud he was of his mama. With a lump in my throat and tears in my eyes, I dedicated 'Stripes' to him. His little face lit up, beaming from ear to ear, as I sang the words over him whilst praying in my heart, 'Oh Lord, let there be healing for my boy.'

PAUSE AND PONDER

What's bubbling to the surface in your heart right now, concerning your own life, your family, your loved ones? I encourage you to write it down. Let it out, bring it to the light of day. As this book progresses, you are going to be given opportunity to bring these matters before the Lord, to do business in the courts of your King, and to bridge the gap on behalf of yourself and your loved ones.

CHAPTER 3

REPOSITIONED

DAYS LEADING UP

I was devastated that we had to pull out of the purchase of our dream home. Sandro comforted me, and reassured me that the time would come, it's just not now. We had the most amazing landlords who allowed us to break our lease when we explained our impending relocation to the USA. In fact, everyone in our community poured into us in ways that we will forever be grateful.

Midwest Charity Begins at Home gave us a generous donation to help cover our costs. Our pastors at our church, Pastor Graham and Cathie Fabian, graciously offered us their home to stay in until the call from the USA came in. Who moves out of their home to give it to someone in need for an undefined length of time?

Friends rallied and helped us pack our lives into boxes. We gave furniture and clothes away just to be able to squeeze everything remaining into one single shipping container to keep our costs down while we were away. Sandro was self-employed at the time, and so no work meant no income. We had an inclination that the cost of living in the USA would be astronomical, and as we were applying for medical visas, we knew we would not be able to work there.

We moved into our Pastor's home on the farm and waited for the call. Our lives had been upended. Somehow the geese and "Bettie" the cow brought comfort to my troubled heart. We made the decision to allow Björn to continue with school until the year ended. Each morning I'd drive the boys into town and drop them off. After popping to the grocery store to pick up supplies, I'd ring my Irish girlfriend Bernadette to see if she was home. She always had the kettle on, and her air-conditioning was spectacular.

I remember this one particular day just after Christmas. It was the hottest day on record, and there was a power cut on the farm. It felt like we were going to be boiled alive. I had reached the end of my tether. When were we going to get the call? How long were we going to have to wait? My piano was in storage, so I couldn't even play, let alone continue teaching. I could however, sing.

A song that resonated in my heart throughout the long and tedious wait was a song written by my dear Auntie Bev's husband, Uncle Kev, before he died. It goes like this:

He Brought Us Out

He didn't bring us out this far
To take us back again.
He brought us out to take us in
To the promised land.

Though there'll be giants in the land,
We will defeat them.
He brought us out to take us in
To the promised land.

I still laugh at how Uncle Kev would now and then replace 'Though there'll be giants in the land,' with 'Those *hairy* giants in the land, we will defeat them.' Despite the frustration and weariness of waiting, we knew there was *weight to the wait,* and so I sang to keep my soul alive.

Whilst writing this part of the book, I felt in my heart to include the song above in my album 'The Wardrobe' as an interlude of honour to Uncle Kev and Auntie Bev, and the impact they had throughout my life.

Scan Code for The Wardrobe

Sandro and I, Ramon and Björn literally had to let go of everything, and each day that passed, we continued to wait.

Finally, the phone rang. I was on the farm alone, sorting through laundry, and despite waiting for this very moment for weeks now, my heart still jumped into my throat. I exhaled for a couple of seconds before answering.

It was the medical team in Perth to say that the hospital in Boston had been in touch. Unfortunately, the stem cell department had shut their doors on their last intake and would not be accepting any further patients. There was no space for Björn.

I literally crumbled to the floor after that call. I lay on the rug in the lounge room of our Pastor's home in a foetal position, cried and prayed. 'What now Lord?' I asked. 'We have literally let go of our whole lives for this opportunity which my boy so desperately needs, and now the door has just been slammed in our faces.'

We weren't in a fit position to make any life altering decisions that day or the next, or the next. We couldn't even bring ourselves to tell the boys, and so we didn't. It felt wrong to put that burden on them. We simply waited and prayed.

About a week later Sandro had popped back to the farm on his way to another job, just to check in and see how I was doing. The boys were at school, and we were sitting in the dining room having a cup of tea when the phone rang. My heart jumped into my throat again. Sandro's eyes widened as he paused to eat his next piece of toast. I closed my eyes, exhaling slowly as I drew the phone to my ear to answer.

It was the medical team in Perth again. My heart pounded so loud it reminded me of practicing scales to my metronome. I had to really focus on the voice on the other end of the line who said something about a hospital in Los Angeles, that had just cut the ribbon on a new stem cell department that had been in the making for the past eight years. Björn had been accepted and would be their very first stem cell patient.

I couldn't believe what I was hearing. Yet at the same time, I knew in my pounding heart that my God was all over this. We had waited and we had trusted. 'Thank you, thank you.' Was all I could say. Sandro hadn't heard the conversation, but I could see the tears of relief in his eyes. He knew. The lady reassured me that the team were prioritising Björn's case, and we would be hearing back within a matter of days.

It was happening. We were heading to Los Angeles.

TOUCH DOWN

The days that followed were a blur. We loaded up the rest of our belongings into the shipping container, and said our goodbyes to our church, school, business and community friends, and family, who had supported us through this whole ordeal. I didn't have the capacity for farewells to be sentimental. All my emotions were wrapped in the wellbeing of my boy, the impending move, and of course the treatment that lay ahead. Saying our goodbye's had to be a matter-of-fact process for me, yet at the same time, I was fully aware that for our friends and family, this was potentially a final goodbye. They didn't know if they would ever see Björn again. There was no guarantee that the treatment would work, and we knew of the risks involved. It was tough seeing our leaving, and the uncertainty of what lay ahead, impact those we loved so deeply.

Before we knew it, we were on our way to Adelaide to meet, for the first time, Dr Nicholas Smith, the Neurologist who had put Björn forward for the clinical trial. Turns out he was from Epping in the UK, just down the road from where we lived and where I'd catch the train into work. At one point during his review of our boy, he admitted that had Björn fallen ill in the UK, he probably would have died. We were very lucky to have been living in remote Western Australia where medical care was prioritised over the big cities. Little did we know that six and half years after our move to Australia, we would be thanking God yet again, for plucking us out of the UK the way He did. Several tests and more paperwork later, we were ready for our onward flight to Los Angeles. We flew via Auckland to break up the travel time and finally arrived in Los Angeles with butterflies in our tummies.

The medical team arranged for a car to pick us up from LAX, and I remember as soon as we stepped outside looking like hillbillies from remote

Western Australia, though it was still winter, the warmth of the Californian sun kissed my cheeks, bringing much comfort to my weary mama's heart. It had been a whirlwind few months, and it was crazy to think that just six months ago we were in Nashville recording an album.

As we gazed out of the windows of the luxury car that was transporting us, we soaked up the beauty of the famous palm trees and ooh'd and aah'd at all the big American cars. The banter of my boys brought comfort, but soon dissipated into the distance, as the niggle in my heart reminded me of why we were there in the first place. I looked over at my sons and could feel the tears begin to well up. 'Oh Lord,' I prayed softly, 'Protect my Björn and give us all strength to face what is ahead.'

Before long, we were pulling up outside the Royal Palace, a rather grandiose name for a beige, two-star hotel in Westwood. But at least we had a bed for the night, and a cosy one at that. We did laugh when the receptionist didn't know what a kettle was. We soon learned that the drink to be had first thing in the morning was drip coffee, not tea.

The following day was Saturday. We were up with the birds and exuberantly headed out to Denny's for a proper American breakfast. Our first official cup of tea was most peculiar. We received teacups filled with hot water, a pile of teabags and slices of lemon. The waitress paused at our request for milk. She politely obliged and returned with steamed milk. Let's just say we didn't have tea that day either!

The rest of the day was spent exploring what was to be our new neighbourhood. We discovered the beautiful apartment block we'd be moving into for the duration of our time there. It was just up the road from the hotel, and there were several grocery and homeware stores in the vicinity. We'd pop in, to gaze at all the weird and wonderful products that we'd never seen before. We took much delight in the American accents, repeating certain words as we attempted to sound the same.

We visited the University Library where Ramon would do his homeschool program for his final year. We discovered the cafeteria and sat down to Panda Express. (A fast-food chain specializing in American Chinese cuisine. Let's just say their Orange Chicken is a big hit in my family!) With full bellies we walked the route to the hospital, so Ramon knew where to find us at the end of his day. The grounds were magnificent, and we all felt safe.

I'm grateful that before our move to the USA, I had reached out to several churches letting them know that we were coming and would be walking into a challenging season and could really use their prayers and support. One church replied and even offered to pick us up for our first Sunday in town.

We were ready at the crack of dawn and were waiting outside the Royal Palace Hotel. A blonde, blue-eyed beauty picked us up. Her name was Heidi.

The minute we walked through the doors of the church, I knew we were surrounded by love. We were welcomed in with open arms and ended up staying the whole day. It thrilled my heart to see Ramon and Björn looking so settled and safe already. People surrounded them wanting to hear their stories, and I caught glimpses of some laying their hands on Björn's head to pray for his impending treatment.

Sandro and I basked in the atmosphere, enjoyed meeting and greeting new people, and during the worship, I felt the warmth of Father God's embrace. We all felt a sense of home away from home. How magnificent and powerful the church is when she does what she is purposed for.

That night we arrived back at the hotel, fired up and ready for the week ahead. Monday's agenda included reporting to the medical team first thing for a meet and greet, and to go through paperwork for Björn's admission. That afternoon we would be moving into the apartment that had been set aside for us. There was an air of excitement, as well as apprehension.

We really didn't have any idea as to what lay ahead.

INDEMNITY FORMS

Walking through the entrance of the hospital, with its vast floor-to-ceiling windows and spiralling staircases, my heart began to pound in my chest. It was hard to comprehend just how much had happened within such a short space of time, that had led us to this very moment.

Only six months ago we were in Nashville recording an album. We had arrived back in Western Australia ready to get my music on the road, when three months later, our lives were upended by our son's diagnosis. And now here we were, about to embark on the most treacherous journey our family had ever faced, and one that would leave us forever changed.

The Doctors shook our hands as they greeted and welcomed us to the United States. Their eyes, however, were fixated on Björn. They walked us all through their new Stem Cell Department, with their state-of-the-art equipment. Doctors and nurses lined up to greet us. As our discussion unfolded, it became apparent that Björn was a living, breathing miracle. Adrenoleukodystrophy does not usually allow life beyond the age of seven. The fact that the illness lay dormant throughout our time in London was miraculous. Even more so, when you know what we as a family had already faced back then, as depicted in 'The Orange Hue.'

After the tour of their new stem cell department, we arrived back at the Lead Doctor's office where he signalled for us all to sit. He and the team were astounded at Björn's responses to their questions. Though he had lost a lot of weight, and his complexion had darkened considerably in the last three months, his mind was sharp, and he was full of cheek and wit. The team adored him already.

Then, as if choreographed, the Lead Doctor signalled to one of the nurses with a frank expression, and she promptly responded by offering Ramon and Björn a bite to eat, to which they did not refuse. She escorted them out, closing the door behind her. I was not prepared for the brutal shift in conversation.

The treatment was not going to be a walk in the park. There were multiple stages involved, and as the Lead Doctor proceeded to explain each stage in detail, I could feel my mama's heart begin to wither at the ruthless reality before us. Sandro grabbed a hold of my hand as we painstakingly endured two hours of medical lingo that I really didn't want translated into layman's terms.

The Medical Board had a duty of care to ensure that we had a full understanding of what Björn as a patient, and we as a family, were about to walk into. This is when the indemnity forms were brought out. Each stage required our signatures to ensure that we would in no way hold the medical team responsible should our son die in the process.

The excitement and energy that I had woken up with that morning was gone. The reams of paperwork to sift through and sign were overwhelming. The reality was that our boy could die from as early as stage one. We had to accept that we could be returning to Australia with our boy in a body bag.

I closed my eyes for a moment and took a deep breath in. Immediately I felt the comfort of Holy Spirit and was reminded of the dream that Sandro had had the night we'd received Björn's diagnosis. As we sat signing, I was quietly singing, 'O the blood of Jesus. O the blood of Jesus. O the blood of Jesus. It washes white as snow.'

WHITE AS SNOW / TRANSPLANT DAY

Björn was responding well to the initial stages of treatment. When it came time for him to commence chemotherapy, Sandro shaved his own head and then shaved Björn's. It was confronting, but necessary, and in fact, Sandro's bald head somehow brought a strange sort of comfort.

We all got into a solid routine. We'd be up at six o'clock to shower and have breakfast before heading to the hospital. We'd then wash our hands and get masked up before joining Björn in his isolation ward. Ramon would pop in for a short while to see his brother. and then would make his way to the University Library to commence his day of studies.

Sandro and I would rotate the afternoon and evening shifts. One of us was always at the hospital, and on the odd occasion when Björn was struggling, one of us would sleep over.

As we were on medical visas, neither of us could work. Having said that, we certainly didn't have time for it. Our days were full. We got involved with church, which really became a lifeline and kept us going. Sandro and Ramon joined the setup crew, and I joined the band, and often played piano or led worship on Sundays. The youth leaders would Facetime Björn so he could enjoy the music from his bed. As soon as we'd get home from church, we'd speed-walk with excitement to the hospital to smuggle in Cheetos and share the day's events, whilst giving Björn big cuddles from everyone who had sent their love.

Most weekdays I'd be sitting by Björn's bedside making pastoral care calls to people who had written in with prayer requests. Little did they know that whilst we were praying for them and their needs, we were also praying and believing for ours.

We'd gotten our hands on a keyboard which we set up in the isolation ward so that we could saturate the room in music and laughter. Ramon brought with him the guitar we'd purchased him in Nashville, and most evenings were spent singing and playing together. Björn's favourite show on the TV was "Diners, Drive-In's and Dives."

I'm no doctor and therefore won't be going into the detail of how stem cell transplant works, but what I can say is that Björn's body was now ready for transplant day. Twenty sixth of March 2015 Björn was given a strong dose of medicine that made him drift into la-la land. As we waited, I began to sing 'O the blood of Jesus' once more. It was a song that had stuck with me from the time Sandro had his dream.

When the doctors arrived with a case of liquid nitrogen housing Björn's new cells, I found myself becoming quite emotional. My mind raced back to when my brother fell ill. Oh, how medical science had advanced since then. But then I felt a wave of anger come over me. How dare this illness take up residency in my family's bloodline. How dare it take my brother's life and dictate my son's wellbeing. My thoughts were abruptly interrupted.

The team were fully dressed in protective face gear, loose fitting overalls, boots and insulated gloves. After several steps and checks, it was now time to undertake the transfusion.

The Doctor unlocked the casing and as he opened the lid, the most majestic, visible fog poured out. If we were going for theatrical, it totally worked. In fact, the whole scene took my breath away. Sandro and I sat in awe at what was happening before our very eyes.

And then, the moment we had all been waiting for. With a large pair of tongs, the Doctor very gently and slowly pulled out this little pouch of blood cells. I gasped whilst placing my hand on my heart. Sandro and I simultaneously stood up.

The cells were pure white.

I was at a loss for words at the sight. Suddenly I was overcome with thoughts of Sandro's dream. The line from Jesus's side going straight into Björn. The song 'O the blood of Jesus, it washes white as snow.'

Could it be that this hereditary blood disorder found in our family's bloodline ended now? Is it possible to break generational sickness, sin and curses through the cleansing blood and power of Jesus?

Yes! And that's why I've written this book, because I am going to show you how.

BLEEDING OUT

The transplant had been a success but the days that followed were critical.

Already we had noticed the effects of the chemotherapy setting in. No one prepares you for the hair loss. Björn's skin was severely itchy, and his sore throat had become so unbearable, the doctors had to prescribe Morphine twice in a matter of just a few hours.

I knew that the objective over the next few weeks was to make Björn as comfortable as possible. The doctors had implemented preventative treatment to avoid infection. He was not allowed any visitors other than the three of us, and as I write this, I'm skimming through my journal from the thirty first of March 2015 where I wrote, 'It's hard watching on the sidelines being unable to take it all away. Even my attempts to comfort him seem futile. Your strength Oh God. Your strength.'

It was my shift, and I made my way to the hospital, only to arrive to commotion in Björn's ward. I hastily washed my hands and put on my mask, pausing at the door to take in a deep breath before entering. There were doctors and nurses everywhere. As soon as I caught a glimpse of Björn violently shivering, I knew he was not okay. My heart was racing, and I suddenly felt ill-equipped to cope with what was happening before me. I could feel the colour drain from my cheeks.

Björn's temperature had climbed to forty degrees, and he was writhing in agony. Then the blood nose started, and it wouldn't stop. The clotting was horrific, it literally looked like he was bleeding out. The sound of the doctors and nurses all talking over each other, and the pace at which they scrambled around his bed, made me feel like I was trapped in a nightmare I couldn't wake up from. Then, he let out the most blood-curdling scream I have ever heard. He clutched his head as if desperate to squeeze out the pain. I couldn't handle the sight and sounds before me. My heart was in tatters, and I just wanted to take it all away from him.

I stood completely helpless in the corner of the room staring in shock at the chaos that reigned. Suddenly my mind raced back in time, to Harlow in Essex, where Sandro was driving as fast as he could to get me to the hospital. This baby was on the way and the contractions were coming in fast. Every speedbump was a gamble. Oh, and then the moment I held my boy for the very first time.

Next thing I'm in Geraldton, Western Australia at the skatepark, watching with one eye as he plummets down the ramp with absolutely no tolerance of fear. Then I'm driving past him and his mates as they line up 'pot plants for sale' along the roadside. All painstakingly and meticulously planted in the heat of the noon day sun, with weeds that they'd planned to sell to the neighbours.

He loved bodyboarding and the day Sandro came home with his first KTM Motorbike, he was the happiest kid alive. He'd light up any room he walked into with his bright chocolate brown eyes that exuded adventure. He would send you into fits of laughter and would drive you completely mad by the amount of energy he still carried at bedtime. To call this kid a power packed, feisty daredevil, was an understatement.

Fast forward thirteen years, which literally shot by in a blink of an eye, with his helpless frame sprawled out on a blood-stained bed surrounded by scared, exhausted and devastated doctors, when I'm tapped on the shoulder.

My eyes are bloodshot from the tears I didn't even realise were pouring out of me. Slowly the doctor came into focus as I looked up at his concerned face staring back at me. 'Nalini, you need to get Sandro and Ramon here right away.'

I will never forget his expression, his words, or the tone of his voice for as long as I live. I could feel fear gripping me from the tip of my head to the soles of my feet, as I shakingly reached for my mobile phone to dial Sandro's number.

My tear-filled-eyes were fixed on my boy as I waited for Sandro to answer. My mind began to race. Is this it? Is this how it ends? Am I calling Sandro and Ramon to come and say goodbye?

I had to force myself to shut off those crippling thoughts or I literally wouldn't have been able to function. Sandro picked up, with concern in his voice. We both knew to *always* pick up if calling from the hospital.

'Babe,' I said quakily. The cough that followed was to try and shake off the fear in my voice. 'You need to come. Get Ramon too.' Sandro didn't ask questions. He would have known that this was serious.

They had managed to stop the bleeding, and the increased dose of morphine had sent my boy to sleep. There is nothing more devastating for a mother than to watch her child suffer and there be nothing you can do to save them.

What sheer relief I felt when Sandro and Ramon walked into the room. It felt like the cavalry had arrived and I could finally exhale. Sandro held me close, then Ramon gave me the biggest squeeze. Oh, what strength their presence brought me that day.

Ramon stood at the end of Björn's bed in a strong and authoritative stance. He didn't look like my little boy anymore. He was now a young man. Sandro sat beside Björn and took his frail hand in his. 'You're going to be okay my boy, you are going to be okay.' My eyes filled with tears as I took a step back to breathe and decompress from the trauma of the day. My Björn was sound asleep. The bleeding had stopped. The doctors continued to monitor his levels closely throughout the rest of the day and well into the night. The worst was behind us.

Or so we thought.

PAUSE AND PONDER

What have you faced in your own life, where it felt as though you were at the end and would not make it through? You see, society tells us to 'Toughen up.' To 'Get over it,' and 'Move on.' But there is nothing more powerful than your own personal story.

So, take a moment to pause and ponder. Recount scenes from your own life and remind yourself of how far you have actually come.

CHAPTER 4

REPOSITIONING

TELL ME ABOUT LONDON

Strong bonds are created when you face a life-altering situation surrounded by loved-ones and people you've only just met. Of course you have to let people in, in order to truly experience the impact of such overwhelming support. But when you do, it's breathtaking and the strength drawn from a text message to see how you're tracking, a phone call, a cuddle, a listening ear, it all adds weight and helps to keep your head above the water till the storm passes.

One of those loved ones for me was the very same lady who picked us up on our first Sunday in Los Angeles, Heidi. She headed up Pastoral Care in the church that had embraced us and walked with us through several weeks of hospital life.

We still had no idea how long the treatment was going to take, and I found myself mentally, emotionally, physically and spiritually exhausted when I woke up to a text message from Heidi asking, 'How about dinner tonight? I'll pick you up.'

It was a welcome breath of fresh air. I had a reason to get out of my usual hospital attire of tracksuit pants and sweatshirt, whipped on some lipstick which I hadn't done in ages, and waved Sandro and Ramon goodbye. I headed out for dinner whilst they headed back to the hospital to spend another evening with our Björn.

The restaurant was magnificent. It was somewhere in West Hollywood and was surrounded by ferns and water fountains. We pulled up and the valet opened our doors. I felt like royalty as we were ushered to our seats. The lighting was soft and ambient. The music provided the perfect backdrop to the gentle hum of patrons' voices, all enjoying the atmosphere whilst sipping on their wine.

We sat down and after a few giggles and light banter, we ordered our mains and raised a 'cheers' to our night out together. We took a sip when Heidi blurts out, 'Tell me about London.'

To be honest, it felt refreshing to be asked something other than, 'What's the latest with Björn?' 'How are you, Sandro and Ramon doing?' 'What are the doctors saying?'

As much as London was a big story to unpack, I was quite happy to go there. I basically shared everything that I later wrote in my first book, 'The Orange Hue.'

Heidi listened intently. There were moments where I cried, and she did too. We were both thankful for our pure white thousand thread count napkins that kindly received our tears and mascara throughout the evening. The meal was delicious, and dessert made for a much-needed intermission in our conversation. I shared about the abuse I experienced at the hands of my boss and the only time Heidi would interject, was when she wanted me to go deeper in a particular area or provide examples. 'And that's how we ended up in Australia.' I concluded. I sat back and took a big gulp of my freshly brewed tea.

The restaurant wasn't as busy now. Guests had been trickling out; waiters were cleaning up tables and preparing for the next day. What time is it? Had we been here that long? Heidi didn't look at all flustered or bothered. She was totally present and though I didn't realise it at the time, I have grown to realise that she was exactly who I needed in that moment. London was seven years prior by this point. Our lives had been hastily ushered to Geraldton, Western Australia and that is where God had placed us. If it hadn't been for the need to relocate to Los Angeles, we would still be there buying our forever home. It was Heidi's question that followed, that shifted everything.

'Are you aware that the way your boss treated you was narcissistic abuse?'

I sat stunned for a few moments as I wrapped my head around the bombshell that Heidi had just dropped. She pulled out a folded piece of paper from her handbag, opened it up and passed it to me asking if any of the behavioural patterns looked familiar.

I cannot remember word for word what was written on that scrap of paper, but I do remember observing statements that jumped out of the page like 'Manipulative and controlling, lack of empathy, sense of entitlement, exploitative and lack of accountability.'

The more I read, the more stunned I became.

This was the first time since leaving London seven years ago, that I finally understood what had really been going on there. Heidi prayed for me that night. She broke off every negative word and every curse that had been spoken over me by my boss. She broke off actions taken against me that were not in alignment with God's word or promises for my life.

It was such an unexpected, yet powerful evening and I walked out of that restaurant completely free from the past. I felt lighter. It was as if I had been carrying a weight on my shoulders for seven years and had finally identified it as such. I had no idea that for those seven years I been carrying such deep trauma, and now I was finally able to dump it all at the foot of the cross.

On our drive home, I leaned my head on the window watching the streetlamps whiz past, whilst replaying the night's conversation in my mind. My eyes were puffy from the tears shed and my word-count was spent, but Heidi understood. She played soft music while she quietly prayed. She allowed me time to digest what had happened.

That night was not just about unlocking and letting go of the abuse I experienced at the hands of my boss all those years ago. I felt a strange release of *everything* that we as a family had had to let go of over years, and that had ultimately led my family and I to this very moment in time.

I let go of the trauma associated with having to leave England so abruptly. For years I had felt like my motherland had been snatched from me, when in reality she's still very much a part of me. But in order for me to truly embrace the seasons ahead, I had to let go of the seasons behind.

I let go of the loss in my heart that we couldn't yet buy our forever home but instead had to pack our lives into a shipping-container and move to the other side of the world, with Jesus being our only assurance for our boy's health. A peace came over me as I gazed at the Californian palm trees and Hollywood sign as we continued towards Westwood. One day and at the right time, I trusted that God would open before us our forever home and it would be exceedingly, abundantly above all that we could ask or imagine.

I realised too that night, that as a mother I had to let go of both my sons. Sandro and I had done everything up until this point to raise our boys in the statutes of God, but ultimately our sons belonged to Him first. We were simply His vessels to love, nurture and raise them, but our boys were now walking into manhood and would have to choose for themselves what paths they would take.

Part of that letting go process was learning to trust God with them at a far deeper level. I was confronted with this revelation when Björn was bleeding out. Did I trust my God with my son's life? Would I still follow Him, love Him and serve Him even if his time has come?

Dinner with Heidi that night was not just divine but was a divine appointment. God needed me to meet her in Los Angeles seven years after leaving London, so that she could walk me through a critical healing process that would actually become the catalyst for this very book.

That night I walked away free, and ready for whatever God had for us ahead.

ALL CLEAR

It had been six months since our move to Los Angeles for Björn's treatment. He was stronger and healthier than he'd been in years.

The Lead Doctor called Sandro and I in for a meeting one afternoon to tell us that they were overwhelmingly surprised at Björn's progress and responsiveness to the treatment. He'd had less complications than they had expected and were completely blown away at the stark contrast between the Björn who'd arrived six months prior to the Björn they were seeing that day. My eyes welled up and I felt a sense of peace wash over me as the doctor announced that we would all witness our son walk out of the hospital.

He went on to say that he saw no reason for us to remain in Los Angeles any longer. He informed us that they would begin the process of discharging Björn from their care, and we could finally return home to Australia.

He added emphatically that Björn would need continued medical monitoring and that he would need a team assigned to him to ensure that he was receiving the proper after-care. If anything, it was this statement that made us realise our time in Geraldton had come to an end. The prospect of trying to get Björn the level of care that he needed from a remote country town in Western Australia would demand exhaustive travel, and that was just not something we were willing to put him or our family through.

We were bursting with joy at Björn's recovery, but instead of being ecstatic at the prospect of returning to Australia, we were caught off-guard at how both of our hearts sunk.

As we chatted and prayed throughout the course of the days that followed, we both realised that after everything we had been through in the last six months, Los Angeles had become like home to us. We wanted to stay.

After speaking to an Immigration lawyer and taking time out for prayer and fasting, the Lord made very clear that He did not want us to remain in Los Angeles but also confirmed that our time in Geraldton had come to an end. So, where did He want us?

We decided to sit down with our church leaders in Los Angeles to seek their council on the matter as we had no home to go back to and certainly felt somewhat unsettled. During our meeting, we expressed that we strongly believed our time in Geraldton was done, and that the Lord was moving us on.

The Pastor was thrilled to hear that Björn was nearing the completion of his treatment, but sad too that our time in Los Angeles was coming to an end. This church had become our family, and we longed to remain a part of it. He said we would be a good fit for either their Sydney or Melbourne campuses, and as soon as he said 'Melbourne', our eyes lit up. We both looked at each other with massive grins sprawled on our chops, as we took in the reality that the desire in our hearts to live in Melbourne from the time, we had arrived in Australia was actually about to happen, and our lives were about to experience another drastic change.

We had only ever been to Melbourne once before and it was only for a twelve-hour stopover before our onward flight to the United States for the recording of the "" album just one year prior. For some reason Sandro and I always felt that we would one day end up living in Melbourne. We just figured it would be well after the boys had finished school. Little did we know that since our move to Australia, the Lord had been preparing our hearts. We also had no idea that the question we had asked the boys over a year ago, whilst sitting in Nando's on Russell Street, was in fact a seed planted in their hearts for the moment we sat around Björn's hospital bed as a family, like we had done countless times over the last six months, to ask the question yet again.

'Ramon & Björn, do you remember us asking you guys whether you would like to move to Melbourne one day?'

Björn responded with the exact same squeals of delight as he had the previous year, and Ramon had the very same subtle smirk.

It was settled. Björn had been given the all-clear, our time in Los Angeles was done, and we were moving to Melbourne.

MIRACLE UPON MIRACLE

I will never forget the day our Björn walked out of that hospital. It had been a gruelling yet exhilarating six months. We saw God show up time and time again, and the day Björn walked down those stairs with all the medical staff clapping and cheering in excitement, my heart burst with joy, relief and wonder. We spent the next week packing up and saying our goodbyes, and before we knew it, we were on the long flight home to Australia.

We had no idea how that move was going to happen, especially as we'd had no income for the last six months. The credit card was almost at its limit, and all our belongings were still in Geraldton. What we did know, is that we were going to have to return to Geraldton to sort things out, and to once again, say goodbye.

In the days leading up to our departure from Los Angeles, I reached out to a few people on the ground, letting them know that we were returning home broke, and would have to start over. We asked for prayer, and we saw our community rally once more in ways that still leave us astounded. For example, two weeks prior to leaving Los Angeles we still had no idea where we were going to stay on our return, when I received an email from the boys' school advising us that they had made the school-house available for us to use for as long as we needed it. On our arrival there was a constant flow of teachers, parents and friends, popping in to welcome us home with tray loads of food. Many of Sandro's business clients had waited for his return, and so within days of arriving, the phone began to ring with job requests.

The following two months were a blur. What I do remember, is visiting Melbourne on my own for a week soon after we arrived back in Australia. I needed to get familiar with the lay of the land, and I needed the Lord to confirm to me that we were doing the right thing.

God miraculously provided a host family who knew friends of ours in Los Angeles. They picked me up from the airport and took care of me throughout my visit. By the time I arrived back in Geraldton a week later, I knew without a shadow of a doubt, that this is where God was repositioning us.

Sandro and I looked at our credit card balance and discovered that we had just enough money to book one-way tickets from Geraldton to Melbourne for Ramon, Björn and I. We didn't hang about. I booked the tickets that night and had a solid timeline of one month to pack, sell clear up everything, say goodbye to our loved ones, before starting over, again. There was much to get done before then.

That night I called my host family in Melbourne to say thank you, and to ask them to pray for our move. They asked when we were coming, and when I told them the date, they couldn't believe what they were hearing. It turns out that they had decided to downsize to an apartment in the city because the family home was too big now that their girls were grown and moving out.

It so happened that Ramon, Björn and I were landing the very next day after their move. The family that they had in mind to rent their house had pulled out, and so promptly asked us if we would like to move in. I couldn't believe it. They even offered for us to move in without any deposit or fixed rental agreement until we were settled. When I say we experienced miracle upon miracle, I'm not exaggerating.

We agreed that Sandro would stay on in Geraldton and work to recoup as much money as possible, before closing off the business and joining us in Melbourne. God provided supernaturally for us, right down to the nitty-gritty detail of everything we needed. For example, I knew I was going to need my car in Melbourne, so Sandro got a quote and was told that it would cost four thousand dollars but that we would need to book the vehicle in for pick-up within the next week or it wouldn't arrive in time for the boys and me. The truth was, we didn't have four thousand dollars.

From the time Björn had been carried into the emergency department nine months prior, we had wanted to invite doctor, Dr Dede and his beautiful wife Dawuta Dede, to our home for dinner as a thank you for fighting for our son's life. Finally, it was happening. I had spent the afternoon cooking and preparing, Ramon and Björn helped tidy up the schoolhouse where we were staying and lay the table, while Sandro worked to bring some much-needed money in.

That night, we had the most wonderful time together. We shared stories of our time in Los Angeles and of course they were gobsmacked at how well Björn was looking. I remember asking Dr Dede how he knew what was wrong with Björn when we rushed him into the hospital that frightful day. He went on to share how there was a time when a similar situation had occurred with a family. They had carried in their little girl but by the time the doctors realised what was going on, it was too late and sadly, she passed away.

Dr Dede told us that God brought that little girl immediately to mind when he saw Sandro carrying Björn's limp body into the emergency department, and so he took that as a warning and acted accordingly.

My family and I are so grateful to Dr Dede for being there that day, and for helping save our son's life. He and his wife Dawuta faithfully prayed for us during our time in Los Angeles, and to be sitting across the table from them, after everything that had transpired, was an absolute privilege.

We had a time of prayer together. They prayed the Lord's blessings over our move to Melbourne. They also prayed for Ramon and Björn, Sandro and I, and when they got up to leave, Dawuta handed me an envelope. 'Don't read it now,' she said, 'Wait till we've gone.'

We waved them goodbye, and after clearing the dishes and getting the boys to bed, I opened the envelope to a note that said, 'This is a gift towards your obedience to go to Melbourne.' And there in cash, was four thousand dollars.

STARTING AGAIN, AGAIN

The goodbyes were hard. We had to leave my parents, our church and school community. The boys had to say goodbye to all the mates whom they had spent their most formative years of their lives with. We even had to say goodbye to the Western Australian sunshine, which for me was not that much of a bad thing.

The hardest part was saying goodbye to my Sandro. The last time we'd said goodbye like this with such uncertainty of when we would see each other again, was when I'd boarded the plane at eighteen years of age, to move from Zimbabwe to London. This time, I had the responsibility of my two sons to take care of, one of whom still required extensive medical care, and the other who'd spent his last six months of high school alone in a library in Los Angeles, with no idea of what tomorrow held, and with no friends to face it with. Sandro reassured me as he had time and time again in the past, that everything was going to be okay. As daunting a prospect as it was, I still had a peace in my heart that we were doing the right thing, and that God would direct us.

Nervously and excitedly, we boarded the plane and waved goodbye to Western Australia beneath us. It had been our oasis and our breath, for the past six and a half years. Los Angeles had been an unexpected yet life transformative six months. It not only brought our son back to life, but I had a newfound healing in my heart. And now it was time for a repositioning.

Fortunately, I had connected with a few people from the church in Melbourne during my one-week visit, and so we were received at the airport by a wonderful couple, Joanne and Neil Percy, who remain dear friends of ours to this day.

They drove us to a leafy suburb called Caroline Springs, to the house I'd stayed in with the host family, and there was my car, already parked in the driveway. Immediately it felt like home. I remember walking through the front door, completely blown away at the hand of God's provision. This whole scene was completely nuts. How does this happen? The family had even left us some furniture, including a full-sized pool table in an upstairs games den. The boys figured they must have died and gone to heaven. Not only that, but we also had cosy beds already made up for us, for that night.

To celebrate, I drove the boys to town and together we sat down to dinner at Nando's.

I wish I could say that our move to Melbourne was seamless and magical. It had its moments, but it was also brutal. The same way it felt seven years prior, being uprooted from England, we now found ourselves feeling like we were being uprooted from both Los Angeles and Western Australia at the same time.

I needed to get myself a job in accounting again, as I knew I had to put food on the table. I remember waving the boys goodbye that first freezing cold Monday morning. Ramon had finished school by this point, but Björn was not well enough to return to school yet, and so I piled him up with his Western Australia home-school curriculum which kept him busy throughout the day. There was plenty of food in the fridge and Ramon was on standby to help him if he needed anything.

I remember driving in to the central business district, getting completely lost on the way, and when I eventually arrived for my trial day at a small accounting firm, I realised that what I was going to earn that day would be less than the cost of parking my car.

Halfway through my day the trauma of the last ten months came to a head, and I ended up calling a meeting with the boss, during which I bawled my eyes out. I explained to him that I had two sons at home, one of whom was severely ill, we'd only just moved to Melbourne after a tumultuous few months, and that I was just not ready to leave them yet.

He graciously allowed me to walk out, and I sobbed all the way home. I curled up on the sofa with my boys that night to watch the film Ratatouille, and together we devoured a massive bowl of popcorn.

I don't know why I didn't get the message the first time round, but I ended up heading into the city a couple of weeks later for an interview at the Melbourne branch of the accounting firm I worked for in Geraldton.

I pulled up outside their skyscraper and sobbed again. This time, I didn't even make it to the front door. Instead, I called the lady in HR and apologised profusely for wasting her time, but I was not ready to return to work. I headed straight back home to my boys.

With Ramon having finished school and Björn not being well enough to return to the physical classroom, those first few weeks in Melbourne were very lonely. All we had was each other from day to day. Sandro had moved in with my parents in Geraldton, while he continued to work to raise finance for our new lives, but oh how we missed him.

The boys and I plugged into our new church, but the adjustment was hard. The culture was different, the people were different, everything was different. And in the midst of it, we were grieving. We were desperately missing our loved ones in Los Angeles. The boys were missing their friends more now than ever before. I had no-one, and had to remain strong for my lads, to try and ease the burden of being in a city we knew very little about.

Let's just say that when Sandro called to say he was done with closing things up in Geraldton, we were elated. We flew Ramon back to Perth, where he met up with Sandro, and the two of them together, drove three and a half thousand kilometres across the Nullarbor Plain, to Melbourne.

By the time they both arrived, they were exhausted, but oh the joy of being together again as a family, was overwhelming. The lads excitedly showed Sandro around the house whilst I put the kettle on for a cup of tea. The days that followed felt like we were cocooned. We didn't leave the house. Sandro slept a lot, we played pool and watched movies, we laughed and cried as we told stories of everything, we'd all been through. Two weeks later, Sandro began the process of walking through Industrial Estates in West Melbourne dropping off his business card. We literally had to start over, with no contacts, no leads, no income, nothing.

While Sandro hustled to find work, my days were spent with home-schooling activities and hospital visits. Björn had been assigned a new paediatrician and endocrinologist, with his Adelaide based neurologist becoming a long-term fixture in our lives.

Friday nights I would drop the lads at our church youth group so that they could start making some friends. My heart ached at how hard this process had been for them. When you move into a new community, the locals already have their tribe. They are surrounded by those whom they have grown up with their whole lives. They are fully settled with no uncertainty of whether they belong or not, and unbeknownst to them, aren't even aware that the new kid is desperate for a hello.

My boys would quietly get into the car after youth finished and I'd ask, 'So how was it, lads?' to which they would blandly respond, 'Yeah, it was okay.'

Starting again, again, seemed more brutal this time. How on earth were we going to make this work?

RILED

When the Paediatrician met with Björn for the first time, his first words were, 'Björn, you have experienced more than most seventy-year-olds.'

He wasn't just referring to the impact that the illness had had on Björn's physical body. He was referring to the mental and emotional impact of the diagnosis, the move to Los Angeles, the treatment itself, and then of course having to pack up our lives in Geraldton and move to Melbourne.

The Doctor's blanket-overview of our lives over the past twelve months hit me like a slap across the face. He then asked Björn to wait in the lounge for me. As Björn quietly closed the door behind him, the Doctor looked at me with concern on his brow. My heart sank. What now?

'It's your son's mental health I'm more worried about.' He said, 'I think he needs to see a psychologist.' He wrote out a referral, and I left his office quite rattled. What could he see that I hadn't seen? Björn was still my chirpy boy, despite everything. What was I missing?

It was the longest drive home. I could feel myself getting riled up on the inside as I replayed the Doctors words in my mind.

How dare this illness take over my son's life like this.

He had gone from being this adrenaline junkie, to being told that he could never do impact sports again. A simple knock to the head could reverse the treatment done, or worse, it could kill him.

I felt as though we had to wrap him in cotton wool and live in a constant state of fear on the off chance that this debilitating sickness could rear its ugly head at any point in time, for the rest of our lives. It was suffocating for all of us.

The lump in my throat was growing. It became so uncomfortable; I thought it was going to ooze out through the walls of my neck. I couldn't just burst into tears and have it out with God, because my boy was sitting right beside me.

I looked over at him and smiled as I fought back the tears. He had been so resilient from his diagnosis 'til now. He'd been prodded and poked, had more needles in him in the last twelve months than we'd ever had in our family's lives combined.

I was angry *for* him. Is this it? Is he trapped under the rulership of an illness that none of us can control? Is my son bound to a life-sentence of hospital visits, and living on a knife's edge, just in case this bubbling volcano erupts again? Is this hereditary blood disorder going to continue taking out the boys in our bloodline for generations to come, and what does my God have to say about all of this?

I thought I was going to explode.

What I didn't realise in the car that day, was that God was stirring my heart to dig deeper into the authority we carry in Him, to confront, go to war in the spirit realm, and break everything that holds us hostage.

Back in West Hollywood I had already witnessed and experienced firsthand, His miraculous healing power, when Heidi prayed over me at dinner.

Together we not only broke curses spoken over me, but we also broke the lingering effects of the trauma I had been living with since leaving London seven years prior. That night, I had walked away completely free.

Now, I was walking into a season of personal reflection, prayer, and one of seeking God, in order to truly understand that He not only gives us the authority to break sin and curses, but He also gives us the authority over sickness and *everything* that stops us from living in the fullness of life that He has for each of His children.

PAUSE AND PONDER

What are some miracles that you've experienced along the way in your own life? Take a few moments to give thanks to God for those miracles. I believe there are even more miracles to come for each of us. Let us never lose sight of what God has already done in our lives.

CHAPTER 5

BREAKING GENERATIONAL CURSES

A LIFE ALTERING REVELATION

Everything had changed and nothing made sense.

I had box loads of brand-new albums that had been sitting since the album launch, or should I say, 'farewell concert', that I had no idea what to do with. The last time my music dream came to a halt was when I discovered I was pregnant. I shoved the dream in the wardrobe of my heart, locked the door and threw away the key, to focus on being a wife and a mom.

I thought God had unlocked that dream when I became a Music Director in London, only for it all to come crashing down. By the time I found myself standing on the distant shores of Western Australia, my love of music was dead. The door was locked, and the key had been thrown away once more. Over time, my Precious Jesus began to heal my heart, and when

I finally felt sufficient strength to get back up and try again, I almost lost my son in the process.

Knowing that Björn's mental health was deteriorating, I organised a meeting with a culinary school in the city, to see if they would consider granting him access to their first-year chef program. It would be something for Björn to enjoy alongside his home-schooling.

I was relieved when the school called to say that they would accept him on a part time basis. It meant that Björn would have something to look forward to in his week. We moved into the city to be closer to the school for him, he found a Saturday job working at a little café down the road, and it seemed like there was a glimmer of hope in his heart again.

From the time Sandro arrived and walked through the Industrial Estates in West Melbourne dropping off business cards, his phone hadn't stopped ringing. He went from no contacts, no leads, no income, to working round the clock just to cater to the demand. Ramon stepped in and worked alongside him, and it brought me great comfort knowing that he was spending time with his dad during such an upheaval. On the days that Björn had culinary school, I had a breather from being the stay-at-home wife, mom, teacher, accountant and general dog's body.

I'd hear the door closing behind Björn as he left the house for the train station, and I'd exhale. Making myself a cup of tea, I'd then curl up on the sofa and I'd watch the city begin to wake. It was in these quiet moments that the Holy Spirit began to softly speak to me regarding this hereditary illness that had taken over my son's, and more broadly, our family's lives.

Holy Spirit led me to Exodus 20 where God gave Moses the Ten Commandments. I had read this passage countless times. Even as a little girl I knew the Ten Commandments. Yet I couldn't believe what I was seeing on paper, straight from the Word of God. Here's the portion that jumped out of the page to me:

> *'I am the Lord your God, who rescued you from the land of Egypt, the place of your slavery.*
>
> *You must not have any other god but me.*
>
> *You must not make for yourself an idol of any kind or an image of anything in the heavens or on the earth or in the sea. You must not bow down to them or worship them, for I, the Lord your God, am a jealous God who will not tolerate your affection for any other gods.*
>
> *I lay the sins of the parents upon their children; the entire family is affected – even children in the third and fourth generation of those who reject me. But I lavish unfailing love for a thousand generations on those who love me and obey my commands.'*
>
> *Exodus 20:1-6 (NLT)*

I found myself becoming overwhelmed at the presence of God in my living room. It almost felt as though Papa God was waiting for my Björn to leave for college that day, just so He could speak to me.

What followed was a life altering revelation.

We had inadvertently become slaves to this sickness, and were giving it power by elevating it ABOVE God Himself.

'That's a little dramatic.' You might be thinking.

I disagree.

God was speaking straight into this riled-up mama's heart that had begun to believe that her son was trapped under the rulership of an illness that none of us could control. A mama's heart that believed her son was bound to a life-sentence of hospital visits, and living on a knife's edge, just in case this bubbling volcano erupted again. A mama's heart that believed this hereditary blood disorder was going to continue taking out the boys in her bloodline for generations to come and that her God was silent on the matter.

The God of this mama was not silent.

He made it very clear to me that day, that I must not have any other god but Him. That it was time to dethrone this illness and break it's curse off me, my son, and our generations to come, because this illness was not welcome here.

A hereditary illness is a generational illness. Verse 4 says,

*'I lay the sins of the parents upon their children; the entire family is affected – even children in the third and fourth generations **of those who reject Me**.'*

We are not a generation who rejects God. Therefore, His promises upon those who do not reject Him, are valid. Verse 6 says,

'But I lavish unfailing love for a thousand generations on those who love Me and obey My commands.'

Immediately Papa God reminded me of my great grandma's death, my grandma's death, and my brother's death, and I realised that this illness had taken out generations before me. He then showed me my Björn, and the dream that Sandro had of Jesus's blood being pumped into Björn's blood, and I knew that God was showing me that this generational curse stopped here, and that we are the generation to break it.

A CURSE BORN

While I knew it was on our generation's watch to break the curse of this illness on our family's bloodline, I didn't know how it got there in the first place, let alone how to get rid of it.

And so began a journey of shutting out the noise, to listen intently to my Papa God's voice on the matter. I asked Him to reveal how the curse came upon my family's bloodline, and what we needed to do to go about breaking this curse once and for all.

What I am about to share with you will bring revelation into your own life concerning curses that may exist, and the authority that you carry to break those curses. Once you understand your position in Christ Jesus, you will not be limited to only breaking the curses on your current generation, but you will be able to break the curses for a thousand generations in your bloodline to come.

Let's begin.

In answer to my question of how the curse of generational sickness came upon my family in the first place, Papa God took me back to the following passage:

> '...I lay the **sins** of the parents upon their children; the entire family is affected – even children in the third and fourth generation of those who reject me. But I lavish unfailing love for a thousand generations on those who love me and obey my commands.'
> Exodus 20:5-6 (NLT)

It was clear as day.
The curse was a direct result of **sin**.

The sin of the great, great grandparent, the great grandparent, the grandparent, the parent, is all passed down to the third and fourth generation in the form of a curse. In other words, the sin needs to be repented of, in order for the root of the curse to be cut.

I had no idea what sins had occurred in the previous generations that resulted in this generational curse. But my God did. And as I continued to seek Him for answers, He continued to speak.

I began to study blessings and curses in the Bible, and eventually the Holy Spirit led me to a most powerful portion of scripture that changed everything.

> *'Now what I am commanding you today is not too difficult for you or beyond your reach. It is not up in heaven, so that you have to ask, "Who will ascend into heaven to get it and proclaim it to us so we may obey it?" Nor is it beyond the sea, so that you have to ask, "Who will cross the sea to get it and proclaim it to us so we may obey it?" No, the word is very near you; it is in your mouth and in your heart so you may obey it.'*
> Deuteronomy 30:11-14

How beautiful is our God to settle one's heart on a matter that you're seeking His council on, where He reassures you from the get-go, that you are more than capable of understanding what He is about to reveal to you.

In the following section God is clear as to where He stands with His people, and He lays out their options:

> *'See, I set before you today life and prosperity, death and destruction. For I command you today to love the* LORD *your God, to walk in obedience to him, and to keep his commands,*

> decrees and laws; then you will live and increase, and the LORD your God will bless you in the land you are entering to possess.
>
> But if your heart turns away and you are not obedient, and if you are drawn away to bow down to other gods and worship them, I declare to you this day that you will certainly be destroyed. You will not live long in the land you are crossing the Jordan to enter and possess.'
> Deuteronomy 30:15-18

Isn't it interesting to see how there is a direct correlation between obedience and blessing? But oh, my goodness. This last portion totally blew my mind:

> This day I call the heavens and the earth as witnesses against you that I have set before you life and death, blessings and curses. Now **choose life**, so that you and your children may live and that you may love the LORD your God, listen to his voice, and hold fast to him. For the LORD is your life, and he will give you many years in the land he swore to give to your fathers, Abraham, Isaac and Jacob.
> Deuteronomy 30:19-20

Whilst I didn't know the details of the sins that had occurred in the generations before me, God knew the details. All He needed of me was to choose whether my bloodline would continue under the curse of the previous generations sin, or whether I, on behalf of my bloodline, would choose life.

The sin had caused the curse, but as a child of God I understood the authority given to me by my Father in Heaven, and that I could stand up, make a decision on behalf of my family and the generations to come, to ensure that we would no longer fall under this curse of sickness, but instead, repent from the sin on behalf of the previous generations and believe that our God would cut off the root of the curse because of our repentance.

Wow. You may need to read that again. You may need to highlight it, underline it, re-write it, bury it in your heart, until it becomes a revelation within you that YOU TOO carry the same authority, through Jesus, to break generational sin and curses within your family bloodline. You are reading this book because God wants to use YOU to be His vessel through His Son Jesus, to bring freedom, healing and restoration, by bridging the gap for you and your family.

A CURSE BROKEN

Despite not being able to identify the specific sin, knowing that my God was fully aware of what had transpired in the generations before me was enough for Sandro and me together, to come boldly before His throne room, and to repent on behalf of the generations before us.

Matthew 18:18-20 is clear:

> *'Assuredly, I say to you, whatever you bind on earth will be bound in heaven, and whatever you loose on earth will be loosed in heaven. Again, I say to you that if **two of you agree** on earth concerning anything that they ask**, it will be done for them by My Father in heaven**. For when two or three are gathered together in My name, I am there in the midst of them.'*

Sandro and I both knew that this matter needed to be brought before God and dealt with once and for all. And so, we did. Our prayer went something like this:

'Dear Heavenly Father,

Thank You for Your love for us. Thank You for revealing to us through the power of Your Holy Spirit the sins of the generations before us and the impact of those sins on the generations since.

Father, whilst we don't know all the details, You do. And so, we come before You with humility of heart, and we repent of all the sins that have taken place within our family bloodline. We ask for Your grace, mercy and Your forgiveness. Your Word promises us that You will lavish unfailing love for a thousand generations on those who love You and obey Your commands.

We love You Lord and we are committed to serving You all the days of our lives. Thank You that You have broken these curses, You have cut the roots and Lord, we give You all the praise and all the glory. Thank You that this sickness will not touch the future generations of our bloodline. It ends now, in Jesus Name, Amen.'

Immediately I felt a release. Like a weight had been lifted. In fact, it didn't feel too dissimilar to how I felt after Heidi, and I had prayed that night in LA.

I knew in my heart that we had brought the burden of this curse before our God, we had laid it at the foot of the cross, and we were now free.

After our time of prayer together, Papa God reminded me of the following passage. Whilst Sandro put the kettle on, I read it out loud.

> *'If My people who are called by My name will humble themselves and pray and seek My face and turn from their wicked ways then I will hear from heaven and will forgive their sin and heal their land.'*
> 2 Chronicles 7:14

It felt so good washing our home with God's word and reminding ourselves of His promise towards us, His children.

A NEW DAY

Nothing had physically changed. Björn was still not well enough to return to school full-time and carried on with his home-schooling. He was enjoying going to culinary school once a week and loved his Saturday job. We still had regular hospital visits, and the results of his blood tests still proved his need for continual medication.

However, everything had changed in the atmosphere around us. We no longer lived under a heavy, burdensome weight, and I knew in my heart that the sickness had been dethroned and its root cut within our bloodline.

Our God was very much on the throne in our lives, and hope was renewed once more. So much so, I found myself venturing into a whole new arena of hosting house concerts. We launched what we called 'Un-Wined' and 'Positivitea' where guests got to experience evenings of cheese and wine or afternoons of high teas, in the surrounds of our new magnificent rented? Tudor home. After nibbles and chatter, we would all gather around my piano where I would share stories intertwined with music. It was off the back of these gatherings and requests by guests, that 'The Orange Hue' was penned.

By this point, Björn had been approached by a top restaurant in the city, to work as a trainee Chef. They had agreed to facilitate his continued studies. It was an opportunity he just couldn't miss, and so he said his goodbyes to the little café down the road and began grinding in the big leagues.

We were all very excited for him, despite the little niggle in my mama's heart. The shifts were long and gruelling on his body, even in those early days, and so I tried my best to keep a close eye on him, which wasn't easy when my boy was seventeen and teetering on the edge of adulthood. He wanted his independence and didn't need mummy nagging on the sidelines to take his medication and get proper sleep.

Sandro and I were Service Pastors at our church, and we were heavily involved. We loved every moment and had the most amazing team working alongside us. The pace was intense, with back-to-back services, and by the time we got home on Sunday nights, Ramon would be gaming with his mates, and Björn would still be working.

Our boys had struggled to find their place in church, and it broke my heart. But as parents, it's important to remember that our function is to raise our kids in the statutes of God, and that eventually, they will need to grab a hold of God for themselves. They cannot live their lives on mama and papa's faith alone. As hard as it was, we knew this, and so we had to let go of our expectations and desires for them, because if we didn't, we would only end up pushing them further away.

As time went on, the niggle in my heart that something was wrong, grew. On the days when Björn was off work, he'd sleep for hours on end, and justifiably so. But when awake, he became more and more withdrawn. Any attempt at a conversation would go from zero to a thousand in a matter of seconds. He was angry and agitated, and we put it down to teenage hormones and the internal wrestle for independence. What we didn't realise was there was a volcano bubbling under the surface that was about to erupt.

THE PHONE CALL

Sandro had popped home for lunch. It was a rare occurrence, as work was extremely busy, and his workshop was on the other side of the city. Today however, he felt the need to come home and spend some time with his wife.

The atmosphere at home had been tense. Things were not good between us and Björn, and any tension between us unsettled me to no end.

Sandro knew I was struggling. That's one of the things I love about him. Whilst he's an incredible businessman and entrepreneur, he's attentive to my needs, and takes really good care of me. Sandro, if you do read this book, I love you, Babe. Thank you for loving me the way that you do.

I had been working on my book, 'The Orange Hue,' when I heard Sandro unlock the front door. I ran downstairs to greet him. It was such a lovely thought that he'd driven all the way across the city to surprise me for lunch. He put the kettle on, and we rustled up a bite to eat before we sat down together in our beautiful ornate dining room that still had blossoming flower arrangements from the previous Saturday night's "unWined" event.

Oh, how I loved this Tudor house with its steeply pitched gabled roofs, its magnificent red brick, and elaborate chimneys. I would wake each day feeling nostalgic as I reminisced growing up in the Tudor style manse back in Zimbabwe, in my childhood years with its arched doorways, the heavy beams and cosy fireplace.

I couldn't believe that I got to live in a house like this. It was a miracle at how we got it in such a short space of time. The only reason we were looking to move from the city was so that we could facilitate larger gatherings. I remember pulling up outside on viewing day when I turned to Sandro and said, 'This is it.'

The winter sun trickled in through our lead windows. We were chatting about the weekend, and catching up about things on the work front, when Sandro's phone rang. I could tell by his expression that he was surprised at who was ringing. He finished his mouthful and grabbed a quick sip of tea before answering.

Isn't it funny at how you build a narrative in your mind of what's being said simply by expressions and responses? We are such curious creatures.

Sandro didn't say much on this call, and he didn't give away as to who it was. He listened. He expressed his gratitude and understanding that it wouldn't have been easy to make the call, and that he really appreciated the courage taken to do so.

I of course, sat with my heart in my throat, wondering what on earth was going on.

Sandro finished the call and shoved in another bite of his lunch. I knew he did this just to give himself an extra moment to gather his thoughts.

My tummy was churning.

Slowly, Sandro began to waylay the message. The call had come from Björn's friend, Chef Massimo. The two had met while working at a café together and had grown close over time. A talented gourmet chef, Massimo would hustle hard in top restaurants until his body would give way. When exhaustion set in, he would step back and find work in small cafés till he regained his strength – only to dive back into the face lane once again. In fact, it was Massimo who had secured Björn's job in this incredible restaurant, and we are deeply thankful to him for being a true friend during some of Björn's most challenging times.

Okay, but why was he calling Sandro?

I could tell by Sandro's sensitivity, that he was doing everything he could to soften the blow for me.

Björn had been skipping shifts. In fact, the restaurant had even received calls from the college to say that he had been missing classes. It didn't make sense. Where was he when he was out for long hours throughout the night, implying in his texts that he was at work?

It was what followed that sent shivers up my spine. His chef felt awful having to admit what he was about to say, but knew he had a duty of care towards Björn, especially as our son was underage.

I took a deep breath in and held on tight.

Björn had been introduced to weed by his colleagues. It was part of the territory when it came to being a chef and it was inevitable that this would happen. The whole team would be on an adrenaline high from the pace at which they functioned from start of shift to finish.

Once all the guests had gone and the clean-up was done, they would rally in the alleyways, de-brief on the night's events, discuss the who's who, whilst puffing on weed to take the edge off. Unfortunately, he suspected that the weed had taken a hold of Björn, and that he might be in trouble.

My heart stopped beating; my mind began to race, and I slowly exhaled. I couldn't believe what I was hearing.

After everything we'd been through with our boy. Packing up our lives in Western Australia, relocating to Los Angles to fight for his life. The upheaval of our move from Geraldton to Melbourne for his continued care, the process of having to start all over again. The impact of all of that, for my son to now fall into a weed addiction.

I could feel my thoughts spiralling as the tears began to drop like rain. Sandro immediately pulled out his chair and came round to my side of the table. He sat beside me and held me close.

We had no idea what we were walking into.

PAUSE AND PONDER

What are some possible generational curses in your bloodline that have maybe impacted you and your loved ones? Sins lead to curses... You might not necessarily be able to identify the sins of your previous generations in your family, but maybe you are struggling with a sin that you cannot break from, no matter how many times you have brought it before God in prayer.

That's because the sin you're battling with is generational, and therefore the root from the past generations needs to be cut. Once this is cut through the appropriation of Jesus's blood, the curse of that sin on your family line will be broken, and you will step into freedom.

Take a few moments to prayerfully consider whether there is anything impacting your bloodline that could be a direct result of sin from your previous generations. Ask Holy Spirit to quicken your heart to any matters that need to be addressed over the coming days. We don't, however, have to go on a wild goose chase, to dig up rubbish that has already been dealt with before God. When God forgives, He forgives. He washes the slate clean and there's no need to re-visit that which He's already forgiven.

Ask God to shine a light on anything that needs to be exposed. As you tune your ear to His voice, He will speak, and He will make it known.

Then, just like Sandro and I did, bring the matter before God. If this is not something that you can do with your wife or husband, contact your Pastor and ask if they will pray with you. Afterall, the Word of God is clear:

> *'If **two** of you agree on earth concerning anything that they ask, it will be done for them by My Father in heaven.'*
> *Matthew 18:19*

CHAPTER 6

UNRAVELLING

TRANSITION

Whenever Sandro and I sit with parents of teenagers, the struggles are the same. Reality is that for the first sixteen years of your child's life, it's your way or the highway. You determine every step they take, the direction of their education, their extracurricular activities, what relationships they are allowed to nurture, and your voice and influence is strong and prevalent.

However, there comes a time when you can no longer function from the role of parent if you want to maintain any kind of lasting relationship with your kids, who are soon to be adults. Whilst eighteen is the legal age of adulthood, seventeen is what I call *a year of transition*. Not just for the child who's transitioning into adulthood, but for the parents who are transitioning into a new role where the mindset can no longer be 'What I say goes,' but rather, a mindset of, 'Whenever you need me, I'm here to guide and advise.' This new role is that of **mentor**.

Transitioning from child to adult is not easy. Hormones are rampant, pressures at school are beyond anything that current generation parents can even imagine. At the crux of it all, teenagers across the globe are trying to figure out who they are, what their purpose is, and where they belong. Part of that process requires them to find their own voice. Not the voice of mom and dad ringing in their heads, but rather understanding and determining what they believe, and in turn what steps they want to take for their lives going forward. This is not easy when we as parents are fully aware that their neurological development is not where their hormones think they are!

Transitioning from parent to mentor is still critical here, despite the challenges that will be faced ahead. We've gotten into a pattern of being the boss and packing the lunches where everything perfectly fits into place. Transitioning however requires letting go of whatever control you thought you had. It's like the scene of a child's first experience on a bicycle. You must let them go for them to truly learn how to ride the bike. Sure, they will likely come crashing down at some point, but that's the only way that they will learn. The parents are then there to pick them up, dust off the dirt and spur them on to get back up again. Eventually when the child is more confident, the stabilizers are removed.

The same applies in this transitioning process from child to adult, parent to mentor. The parents must start the process of letting go so that their soon to be adult children can start riding on their own, even if it means that they fall sometimes.

For us, it was a brutal transition.

It had been a few days since that disturbing phone call, as we needed time to digest what had been shared, and to figure out our method of approach. There was no easy way of doing this, but in our family, tea always helped. We had a freshly brewed batch sitting at the table when I knocked on our boy's bedroom door for a chat. He had slept most of the morning and was due in for the late shift. He was incensed at the suggestion that he had not been missing shifts or classes at college and categorically denied smoking weed.

Unfortunately, the days and weeks that followed led him further down a rabbit hole that I as his mama, knew he wasn't old enough, strong enough or well enough to navigate. His behaviour was becoming more and more erratic. He would blow up into a rage without warning, pack his bag and leave for days on end without any contact. He'd then come home insisting that he'd been staying with work mates, as he'd had back-to-back shifts. We stayed out of the way for the sake of peace in the house, but the undercurrent was certainly simmering.

We He? had an upcoming appointment with his neurologist Dr Nick in Adelaide that we couldn't afford him to miss. I knew we needed external support as we were just not getting through to Björn, and so I called Dr Nick ahead of our visit and forewarned him of what had been happening. Deep down in my mama's heart I hoped and prayed that our time together in Adelaide would be a good opportunity for me to talk some sense into my boy.

After landing we went straight to the nearby candy store and piled up on goodies for us to indulge on throughout the evening. This had become our little thing to do whenever we had medical appointments in the calendar. Lollies and spicy crisps, preferably Cheetos, which we discovered in America, were all that was required to make everything good again.

Dr Nick was straight down the line. Björn, with his medical condition, could not afford to go down the path of weed or cigarettes, or anything untoward or outside of a balanced nutritious diet, as it could risk the reversal of his treatment and potentially kick-start further degeneration. I hated every second of that meeting. Björn seemed completely numb to Dr Nick's warnings, almost nonchalant, with little to no reaction at all.

Walking back to our hotel that evening, I felt as though I was walking with a stranger. We had walked that route multiple times throughout the last four years. One of my fondest memories was when he got to hang with the crew at the Jamie Oliver restaurant. He had so much hope and excitement for the future then, but today, his head was down, and his mind was miles away.

The distance between us broke my heart. I wished I could take all his anxiety, fears and questions away, but I couldn't. I was completely helpless. He didn't want to talk, and I didn't know what to say, and the gap between us grew bigger and bigger. When he lit up a cigarette outside the airport, I knew then that my attempts at putting out the warnings had proven futile. I wasn't returning home to Melbourne with my little boy. I was returning home with a young man who had decided that it was time for him to choose his own path. How on earth was I to let him go when he was more vulnerable now than he'd ever been in his whole life?

FROM BAD TO WORSE

It was our twentieth wedding anniversary and Sandro, and I were off to Italy to celebrate this incredible milestone. A part of me wanted to cancel the whole trip because of how volatile Björn's behaviour had become. Yet at the same time, there was very little that we could do. The strain on our household was taking its toll, and we knew time apart would probably be the best thing. Our older son Ramon was caught in the middle of all of it, despite his attempts to stay out of the way. He reassured me that he would keep a look out for his brother while we were away, and that we must just have the most amazing time.

As magnificent as Italy was, and as much as Sandro and I tried our hardest to soak up everything there was to see and do, the volcano on the home front had reached explosion point. Calls and texts late into the night from Ramon to say 'Björn hasn't been home in two days' would send me into a state of panic. My spine had become all too familiar with the sensation of chills and shivers. Sandro would very calmly stroke my back and remind me that there was literally nothing we could do from this far away, we must trust God in the process and know that everything was going to be okay.

After Ramon ended up with police at the front door asking questions about Björn's whereabouts, I knew we had to do something. I reached out to my parents and asked if they could take Björn in, just until we got back home. Ramon was not coping with Björn's escalating erratic behaviour, and our anniversary trip was turning into a total nervous-system nightmare. I couldn't eat or sleep, my family was falling apart, and I just wanted to get home to try and piece it all back to together again. My parents were amazing and took care of Björn for the last remaining days of our trip.

We flew back into Melbourne and headed straight home. We had hardly stepped foot in the front door when my parents arrived with Björn. We could tell by their body language, and the fact that they didn't stay for tea, that their coming to the rescue had not been a pleasant experience. Björn smiled when he saw me. His face was drawn, and when he leaned in for a hug, I could tell he had lost weight. I knew he was not okay, and my mama's heart didn't want his hug to end.

The four of us spent the rest of the afternoon catching up together as a family. We curled up in the lounge over cups of tea, and shared stories and photos of our travels, enjoying what seemed like a moment of normalcy. Looking at my boys laughing together brought a sense of relief. Maybe things weren't as bad as they seemed. Maybe things had miraculously shifted while we'd been away. I probably just needed to chill and back off from presuming the worst.

Not too long after family dinner, Sandro and I decided to call it a night as the jetlag had well and truly set in by this point. My heart was settled. Ramon was happy, Björn was home, we were together and that was all that mattered.

I woke with a fright to the sound of Sandro rummaging around for his dressing gown and bedroom slippers. The banging on our front door reverberated around the house and once again, the chill up my spine was back. Something was seriously wrong. I flicked on the light and checked the time. It was three o'clock in the morning and still pitch-black outside. My heart pounded in rhythm with the banging as it continued.

Sandro had already rushed downstairs, and I followed soon after, as chaos reigned in my mind. Who on earth was so bent on our attention at this hour? As I got to the bottom of the stairs, I saw Sandro standing with three policemen. Immediately I found myself doing a family headcount. I knew both Ramon and Björn were home so it couldn't have anything to do with them. There was a momentary sense of relief that came over me, and then one of the policemen began to speak.

He asked if we had anyone living here by the name of Björn Tranquim. My eyes couldn't open any wider as I felt panic set in throughout my whole being. 'Yes,' Sandro replied, 'He's, our son.' The policeman solemnly explained that they had received multiple calls throughout the night advising them that our boy had been posting very dark threats of suicide online, and because of the number and detail of reports they had received, they had a duty of care to sight him.

I felt as though my body was going to give way. My head felt light; my breathing laboured. Oh, my boy, my precious boy. My mind raced to his bedroom door behind me. There was no way I would be able to bring myself to open his door. The policeman sternly, yet sensitively, looked at me and said, 'Ma'am, we need to sight your son.' I froze. Sandro froze.

'Please direct us to his room,' he said, giving me a nod of comfort that reassured me that they were going to deal with this, and that we didn't have to. I mustered up enough strength to point in the direction of our boys' bedroom, as Sandro and I stood fixed in a complete state of shock.

The memory of this moment is still etched in my mind as if it happened only yesterday. It is a scene I hate to recount. I must be honest that this book has not been an easy for me to write. Penning these words has required me to revisit scenes like this, almost as though I have been reliving them all over again, in order for me to explain to you what happened and how it felt. Why? Because it will evoke the unlocking of doors in your own heart as you too revisit scenes in your own life, that have maybe left their mark. It's only as we unlock those doors and face the rooms filled with clutter, that we are able to slowly and gently work through the mess, in order to reach the window. Where we can draw back the curtains and feel the warmth of the sun on our cheeks. opening the latch, swinging the window wide, and allowing a gentle breeze to begin to permeate the room. Hope is renewed as the gloves come on and the cleaning can begin.

We were still in shock as we heard voices in Björn's room. I was relieved to hear the faint voice of my boy. Thank God he was still alive. I closed my eyes to restrict the flow of tears. A few moments later, the policemen walked out of his room, closing the door behind them. One of them came straight to me and placed her hand on my shoulder.

'Your boy is okay... for now.' She said gently, 'But he does need help.'

And with that, they thanked us and left.

We didn't move as we stared at each other in bewilderment. At this point, Ramon came out, asking what all the commotion was about. I felt like if I didn't get out of there quickly, I would end up on my knees sobbing. I didn't want to freak Ramon out. He'd been through enough while we were away in Italy, and so I simply blurted out, 'Dad is going to make us all a cup of tea, I just need a moment.' Sandro nodded reassuringly and signalled for Ramon to join him in the kitchen. I ran upstairs into my walk-in-wardrobe, where I fell to my knees with my head down, before burying myself in my winter dressing gown to mute my screams.

My boy was in turmoil, and I couldn't fix anything. After a few moments, I managed to compose myself. My eyes were puffy as I dialled the number for Lifeline. I lay in a foetal position on the carpet of my wardrobe, as the phone rang. A little old man answered. 'This is Lifeline, how may I help you today?' His voice was soothing like that of my dad's. I closed my eyes and resisted the lump in my throat as I brought myself to say, 'My son is suicidal, and I don't know what to do.'

He explained that we needed to get him to the hospital emergency department for a psychological evaluation. Medical professionals needed to determine the severity of his threats, and from there, they would guide and advise as to next steps. As gentle and reassuring as his voice was, the reality in front of us was brutal. There was no avoiding this, no sugar coating it or burying it under the rug in the hope that it would all just go away. This mama was going to have to find courage from somewhere to face this. 'Oh Jesus, help me.'

FULL FORCE

I washed my face in an attempt to prepare myself for the full force of what lay ahead. I made my way downstairs to Ramon and Sandro waiting in the lounge, but there was no sign of Björn. I knocked on his door and when I opened it, he was still in bed. I'm not sure if he thought we were all just going to head straight back to sleep after that bombshell, but we as a family needed to talk, and so I encouraged him to join us. The gentle bribery of a cosy cup of tea brought a smile to his face, and a few moments later he sat between Sandro and Ramon, probably wondering what on earth was going on. There's no instruction manual for what to say when police show up at your door informing you that your son is suicidal. None of us had any idea how to handle this.

In our numbness we reiterated our love for both our sons and reassured them that we were going to get through this together as a family. The little old man's voice from Lifeline rang in my head. At least I had an action plan for that morning. I explained to Björn that we were going to take him to the hospital for an assessment. He seemed happy about that. If anything, his openness to the process only confirmed how severe things had gotten for him. He not only needed help, but he also wanted it. Sandro was under a lot of pressure with the business and didn't have the capacity to join me. Ramon said he would come with us, which I really appreciated as I didn't feel strong enough to do this alone. We prayed together before facing the rest of the day, had a group hug, got ourselves ready and headed out the front door.

The boys headed to the car when I saw our neighbour walking straight towards me at pace. He was angry. I locked the front door, took in a deep breath, and turned to greet him. Without even a 'hello', he landed into me. Björn had been up to no good while we were away in Italy, and this man had reached his limit. Late nights of ins and outs, loud music into the early hours of the morning, and then of course the frequenting of police on our doorstep.

'This is not the sort of demographic we are used to.' he said.

I was not in the headspace to cope with this man's abuse. He was up in my face, and while he had every right to be angry, and I'm sure every word he said was true, this mama bear's boy was in a bad way right now, and I was not going to entertain this conversation any longer.

I held up my hand for him to stop speaking. It was a rather abrupt move on my part, but it got the reaction I was after. He immediately stopped mid-sentence, with his big blue eyes staring back at me questioningly.

He had grey thinning hair and had been a delightful neighbour up until that point. I apologised to him for my son's behaviour, and then firmly pointed out, that we'd had the police on our doorstep in the early hours of that morning to let us know that Björn was suicidal and that I was heading to the hospital with him at this very moment. We would have this conversation at another time.

I could tell my words hit hard, as the colour drained from his cheeks. He patted me on my arm, 'Of course, of course, you go,' he said, as compassion overtook every trace of anger. He watched me walk towards the car and with a sadness in his eyes, he waved as we left.

'Speak up.' the triage nurse blurted out, with irritation in her voice. She didn't look up once as this exhausted mother tried to utter the words clearly but softly, 'My son is suicidal.' I didn't want everyone else in the emergency department hearing of the implosion that was taking place within my family right that moment.

We waited for hours, and eventually my Björn was called through. For 'patient confidentiality purposes' we weren't allowed to be with him. This blows my mind considering I'm his mama, and he wasn't even an adult yet. Ramon and I waited. When he did return, we all left without any word of guidance or support.

I tried asking Björn how it went, and what steps we were to take to get him the help he needed, but he didn't want to talk about it. Ramon remained quiet and in his own thoughts as he gazed out of the car window. We drove home with absolutely no idea as to what we were meant to do now.

The days that followed were a total nightmare. I felt like I couldn't let Björn out of my sight for fear that he might take an overdose or jump the tracks. We stayed home and waited. I cancelled meetings and appointments and felt as though I was on permanent standby. What were we waiting for? I still don't know to this day. Some sort of direction maybe? An underlying hope that the suicidal thoughts would somehow disappear, and that Björn would randomly wake up one morning back to his usual bright-eyed and bushy-tailed self?

Well, that day didn't come. If anything, the waiting, and hovering, with the constant checking in to see if he was okay was actually suffocating him, and all of us around him. It was one Friday afternoon, Sandro came home early and insisted that he and I take a walk. I was at my wits end with lack of direction and support. I wasn't eating or sleeping, and I had no idea how to protect my son from himself.

The walk helped. The solid trees, that had stood the test of time blowing in the breeze, brought a sense of comfort. Neighbours pottering about in their ornate, manicured grounds allowed me to drift into other worlds for a moment. Sandro and I didn't have much room in our cluttered minds to say much, but facing this together was what mattered. By the time we arrived home to put the kettle on, Björn was nowhere to be seen.

Panic stricken, I scoured his room for some sort of a sign. A note or anything that would give me an indication as to where he was. I attempted to call him. He didn't pick up. I tried texting, he didn't reply. Did he have his medication with him? Who was he with, and where would he go when he had no job to go to?

Sandro, Ramon and I sat texting friends to see if anyone had seen him. I reached out to his chef to see if he had come by the restaurant, but he hadn't. I didn't know if Björn had any friends outside of work or church, and if so, who they even were. By midnight I was beside myself with worry. Björn had never done anything like this before. We had always kept in close touch, especially since our move to Melbourne, and with the events over the last few days, I knew he was in an extremely volatile state.

Eventually, with no sightings from friends and family, we decided to call the police to report him as a missing person. The police advised us that we had to wait for a minimum of twenty-four hours before they would take any action. It was a soul-destroying wait. Not one person in our friend's circle had seen or heard from him. Suddenly out of nowhere, Sandro jumped up and said, 'Let's go looking for him.'

The three of us drove the streets throughout the night, as we brought back to memory places that may have held some kind of sentimental value to Björn. We visited Nando's on Russell Street, Melbourne Central Shopping Mall, the Atheneum Theatre, his college, and the restaurant where he had worked and found community for a time.

Nothing.

We all crawled into bed in the early hours of the morning to try and get some sleep. My mama's heart was in turmoil. My son's bed was empty, and my pillow was wet with silent tears. How could this be happening?

On the twenty-four-hour mark, we made the call. Several hours later there was a knock on our door. It was the very same thud as a few weeks prior. My body clammed up at the sight and sound of police once more. Sandro ushered them into the lounge, where they settled themselves in to ask a series of questions. When they were done, they said they would do everything they could and left.

THE VOICE NOTE

I needed to keep busy and so I grabbed my washing up gloves, bin bags and cleaner, stormed into Björn's bedroom, on a mission to have it sparkling clean for his return. I flung back the curtains and swung open the windows to get rid of the stale stench of piled up mugs, plates, empty pizza boxes and takeaway cups, with curdled milk still stuck to the bottom. We had a rule in our house. If you wanted your bedroom to look like a bombsite, your door must be kept shut at all times. Björn's bedroom was a no-go-zone for this mama, and I was fine with it. The closed door kept me out and therefore kept the peace.

Clothes were strewn across the floor; the visual chaos was certainly a reflection of the state of my boy's mind. I picked up an iPad I didn't recognise, and then whilst reaching for more stuff under his bed, I came across a mobile phone.

The all too familiar sensation of chills and shivers up my spine returned once more as I, with unexpected ease, unlocked the handset. There was no pin, there were no saved contacts. Only screeds and screeds of dialled and missed numbers. As I knelt on the floor, surrounded by the silence of my son's absence, I came across a voice note.

Clutching the old handset, I froze for a moment staring at the play button. Do I really want to hear this? Am I ready for absolutely anything. or is there a risk that once I've hit play, more will be unravelled which could potentially lead to my own unravelling? As it was, I felt like I was living on a knife's edge. The not knowing led to not sleeping, not eating. Every phone call, every knock on the door made me jump out of my skin. I was constantly on edge, fully aware of every sound and smell around me. It was like my senses were on high alert.

My awareness suddenly led me to who was at home. Ramon was in his room playing guitar, so there was no risk of him hearing the voice note. Sandro had gone to the workshop to do some sorting. Seems that for both of us, the act of cleaning brought with it a sense of purpose and a bringing to order. He loved being there at the weekend as he had the place to himself. No staff, no clients, no noise, just him, his cars and his thoughts.

My mind didn't have the brain space to think about Christmas being just two days away. I did know that I had a house full of guests coming for Christmas Day lunch, but right now, all I could think about was hitting the play button on this voice note.

I took a deep breath in and slowly exhaled as I hit play and closed my eyes. The scene in my mind set my heart racing. I could hear running. The scuffing of trainers on the pavement. It sounded like the shutting of a car door. I imagined a carpark. Then, the sound of my son's terrified voice as he put out a warning to whoever he was speaking to.

'Get down, get down, his dad is with him! For f***'s sake, his dad is with him!'

Commotion, chaos, scrambling behind cars, when abruptly, the voice note stopped.

I was aghast.

I threw the phone into the corner of the room as if to reject what I'd just heard. I felt sick to the core. Questions began racing in my mind.

What was my son involved in? Who were these people? Who was this person who brought his dad? What were they going to do if the dad hadn't shown up?

As I sat on the carpet of my son's bedroom, a harsh reality hit me. We knew very little about our seventeen-year-old son and his life. We certainly had no idea what was going on, and it was evident that there was much more to the puzzle than we thought. Now the unidentified iPad lying on the bedside table had a sinister connection to an underworld we naively knew nothing about. Still shaking like a leaf, I mustered up the courage to call the family liaison officer who had been assigned to us since Björn was officially reported as missing.

I explained to them the details of the voice note and immediately picked up concern in their tone. Panic stations were alerted once more when they said they would pay us a visit first thing in the morning. Without wanting to disturb Sandro's solace, I waited till he got home to share with him the events of the day. He was as shocked as I was.

My mama's heart was in added turmoil that night. My son's bed was still empty, and my freshly changed pillowcase was wet with silent tears once more.

CHRISTMAS EVE

This was a Christmas Eve like no other. I was determined not to cancel our Christmas plans just because of everything that was happening. My dad's sister was visiting for the first time from Mumbai, we had friends booked in to spend Christmas Day with us, and so I was up at the crack of dawn, finishing off gift wrapping and laying the table, which I always found to be therapeutic.

Sadly, we hadn't hosted any guests in the last couple of months as things had escalated so rapidly. We just didn't have the mental or emotional capacity to entertain. I was devastated to halt my "Positivitea" and "unWined" events but knew deep down that my focus had to be solely on my family for now.

The last of the Christmas preparations were well underway when, there it was again, the almighty pounding on the front door. Chills and shivers shot up my spine yet again, as I closed my eyes and consciously slowed my breathing. As much as I loathed the sensation of dread coursing through my body, I'd rather that, than to have become familiar with police at my door.

I dried my hands, flung the dishtowel onto the kitchen counter, and made my way to welcome my unwanted guests. They greeted me and headed straight in with an air of informality. They'd been round several times in the last few days and had become quite accustomed to my cups of tea. It was Sandro's last day at work before the Christmas break, Ramon had disappeared into his room, and so I braced myself for the impending conversation. We had not heard from Björn since he had left three days prior, and I was beside myself with worry. I had a constant sick feeling in the pit of my stomach, but I had to keep going for the sake of Ramon, Sandro and myself.

The police listened to the voice note repeatedly as a young officer took notes. There were a few interesting looks between them, and the odd conversation in what seemed to be a completely different language. You know how kids sometimes pester their parents to explain what they were just talking about, because parents had learned the skilful art of speaking in stealth-mode? The gentle rumble under one's breath where you both know exactly what the plan is, satisfyingly smirking at each other while the kids have absolutely no idea what's been said. It was a bit like that. Must have been police talk. They were speaking in code, and I was just there, sipping tea, none the wiser, but desperate for answers as to where my son was.

When they were done, they firmly advised me that I needed to draft up a text message to send to every single friend of Björn's that we knew. I had to inform them that Björn was officially missing, and that if they knew anything in relation to his whereabouts, they must notify the police immediately. I was also to add, that if they did know where he was, and chose *not* to inform the police, that they would be perverting the course of justice and could be arrested. It's only now while I write this that I realise the extent of what was actually happening in that moment.

To be honest, I had more contacts for Björn in Western Australia than I did in Melbourne. However, I knew what needed to be done, and so as soon as the police left, I got onto it. I called Sandro and updated him on the morning's events. We both templated messages for not only Björn's friends, but for ours also. It was a far cry from Christmas greetings, as we asked them to bridge the gap in prayer for our missing son. All I wanted was for my boy to be home safe and sound in time for Christmas tomorrow.

A few moments after spamming our contacts, messages and phone calls started pouring in. But it was one text in particular that caught my attention. It was from Björn's mate Tom, who was back in Geraldton. He was there when Björn had first fallen ill, and he even fund-raised and got himself an after-school job, just so he could visit Björn in LA during his treatment. He was a 'no matter what' kind of friend and had received one of my texts.

He was devastated to hear that Björn was missing, and said he would jump onto Snapchat to see if he could trace his whereabouts. My heart skipped a beat at the possibility, and I immediately began to pray specifically for us to locate him that day. Björn's youth leader called. One of the Pastors at our church whom we had messaged had broken the news to him, and he rang to say that he was at work in the city, but if there was anything he could do, to please call him straight away. Ramon was texting friends also. We were all inundated and overwhelmed with all the calls, but in a good way. It was comforting to know that we had the support of so many around us.

Ramon and I had been chatting and replying to text messages when I saw Tom was calling me again. My heart began to race as I picked up, Ramon staring at me in anticipation as to what Tom had to say.

'I know where he is,' he started.

I couldn't believe my ears.

'What do you mean you know where he is?' I asked, pacing up and down my lounge room.

Using Snapchat, he had traced Björn's whereabouts to the Westfield Shopping Centre in Doncaster but asked me not to get too excited. The data was from about an hour earlier and Björn had been offline since. Well too late mate (as the Aussie's say), I was bursting with excitement. This was exactly the kind of lead we had been waiting for.

Oh, the feeling of hope renewed when all hope had been lost, was nothing short of breathtaking. As crazy as this may sound, I knew in my heart the moment Tom's call had come through, that we would find my boy and he would be home for Christmas.

PAUSE AND PONDER

What I've come to realise is, that what was unravelling in our family, was the ramifications of this generational curse within our bloodline. Whilst we knew that the curse had been broken, our son was still dealing with the impact of it within his own life. He had still been diagnosed with this hereditary illness and had left everything he knew and loved, to relocate to the other side of the world, with no guarantees that the treatment would work. Living on a knife's edge of not knowing from one day to the next whether he would live, or die, was hard enough for us as adults to come to terms with, without the unbearable weight for him as a child.

The generational curse brought physical sickness, and now mental and emotional anguish that my boy had been so desperately trying to escape.

Take a few moments to ponder over what is happening in your life right now, that may very well be directly connected to generational sin or curses. You don't need to go on a garbage hunt. Holy Spirit will bring to your memory anything that needs to be dealt with. Jot them down in a journal and keep reading.

CHAPTER 7

BREAKING CURRENT CURSES

HELP ME SEE HIM

Ramon rang Sandro while I called our family liaison officer who said he would get word out to the Doncaster police immediately. I then rang Björn's youth leader and told him that Ramon and I were heading to the mall. He asked for us to wait for him, he was on his way, as he wanted to join us in the search.

It was three o'clock and about forty stinking degrees outside by the time we left the house. The traffic was hideous as of course, everyone was out doing last-minute Christmas shopping. I turned the volume up on the radio as conversation was sparce. We were all in our own world of thought. For me, my tank was running on empty and in my outward silence I inwardly cried out to God for help. 'Oh Lord, help me see him.'

We managed to find a parking space on the roof of the mall, in its carpark that caters for over 5,000 vehicles. It was a good three-minute walk in the scorching sun, evidence alone that this son of mine meant more to me than anything, because *nothing* got me out in this kind of heat, especially when there are crowds involved.

To say it was heaving with people is an understatement. There were people everywhere. We literally couldn't see the ground beneath us. My heart became overwhelmed at the vastness of impossibilities. How on earth are we going to find our son in one of the biggest shopping centres in Victoria, Australia, on one of the busiest shopping days of the year? We are talking 123,165 square meters of retail space spread out over 4 floors.

The three of us looked at each other in dismay. How were we going to do this? As I looked out across the sea of shoppers all hustling for commodity, the mama-bear within me riled up. All that mattered to me was the safety and wellbeing of my son and I didn't care how long it took; I was not leaving this mall until I found him. I messaged Tom to see if Björn had logged onto Snapchat in the meantime, and then the three of us split up. We would cover much more ground doing it individually than together. Each of us had our mobile phones to hand and would ring with any updates. We quickly prayed together, took a deep breath in, and went our separate ways.

Björn had brought me to this mall about a year prior, and I recognised one of the shops he'd taken me into, so I started there. I squeezed between people and sped through every aisle with my eyes darting from one face to the next, but there was no sign of him. My heart was racing, and I knew I carried concern on my brow, but there was nothing I could do about that.

I stood outside the shop for a moment to slow my breathing as I contemplated where to next. People were streaming in like termites oozing from their mound. It was hot even with the air conditioners blasting, and I could feel a rush of panic piercing through my frame.

'Oh Lord,' I uttered softly, 'Where is my boy?' I looked across the way and saw McDonalds. I remembered it from the last time I was here. It had a strange narrow passage with eating booths on either side, and windows overlooking the motorway. I pelted in its direction, scouring every face across my path.

There was an empty booth on the side of the window where I stopped to look out and noticed a bus stop. Immediately I found myself straining to see every person who got on board. Was he on the bus? Where would he be going? I checked my phone to see if Tom had responded, but nothing. I looked up and saw an emergency exit door at the end of McDonalds's strange narrow passage, and before I knew it, I was rushing past devouring eaters, begging God, 'Help me *see* him.'

The strength of the searing heat hit me as I pushed open the doors. Blinded from the glare of the Australian sun, I had no choice but to pause. My eyes took a moment to adjust, when to my right, I saw the bus leaving its stop. I squinted as I tried to focus on each and every passenger and then prayed again, 'Oh God, help me see him.'

I gazed at the pavement for a moment, disappointment sweeping across my face, as I wondered why I had stepped into the sweltering heat, and what I was even thinking to fathom that I would see my son in such an overcrowded mall. As I was about to turn back around and retreat through the emergency doors behind me, I lifted my head and saw three figures about a block away, walking down the hill in my direction.

I did a double take. I felt a cool rush immerse my whole being, from the tip of my head, right through to my baby toes. Are my eyes deceiving me? I rubbed them trying to force them into focus once more. I looked harder and there in the distance was my Björn. I knew his walk; I knew his frame. There was no shadow of a doubt in my mind that this was my boy.

In that moment, I didn't feel the sting of the sun piercing my skin. I let out an uncontrollable howl as the tears gushed forth, and before I knew what was happening, my feet beneath me were running towards him at a speed they had never run before. I yelled out his name as I charged in his direction.

'Björn! Björn! Björn!'

I felt like a lioness chasing the hyenas away from her cubs. My eyes dashed to the two men walking on either side of him. One had stopped by this point. He was staring straight at me, and I knew he didn't like what he was seeing. The other was still at my son's side as he and Björn headed down the hill towards me. My eyes were fixed between the two of them. I felt no fear. Whoever these people were, they were messing with the wrong mama. I knew they knew I was coming for them, but they didn't have time to react. All they could do was watch in disbelief, as this crazy woman roared in their direction.

It was only when I reached arm's length that Björn realised who it was. 'Mom?' He asked softly, in complete disarray. 'What are you doing here?' Awkwardly he looked around him as if embarrassed by my presence.

He was like an emotionless zombie. His eyes were glazed over, and I knew he was high. He seemed hardened somehow, with his hands in his pockets, his chest puffed out. It was as if he was speaking to a complete stranger and vice versa. But I didn't care. He was my boy, and he was safe.

Without hesitation, I flung my arms around him and held him tight. He didn't move. He just stood there like a brick wall. The man who had stopped walking earlier, scurried past us like a hyena with its tail between its legs, and waited near the bus stop. The other just stood in silence, leaving me to my mama moment.

I stepped back from my boy, when the hair on the back of my neck stood to attention as I turned in the direction of the devious, dark-haired individual standing next to Björn. He looked at me as I stared straight into his chocolate brown eyes, whilst announcing in a bold and commanding voice, 'Björn, you are coming home with me.' I grabbed my sons' hand

and headed straight towards the emergency exit that only moments ago I walked out of.

Whoever these two men were, they regrouped and stood staring as I lead my son away. We approached the door, when Björn insisted on saying goodbye to them. I gave him a moment to do so, but I wasn't too far behind. There was no chance on earth that I was going to let him out of my sight.

Before long we were inside the mall, regrouping with Ramon and Björn's youth leader. I could see the relief in their eyes. My heart was bursting, and the adrenaline continued to pump through my veins all the way home.

No one uttered a word. It was an awkward and uncomfortable drive.

I had a sick feeling that this wasn't over.

This was in fact, just the beginning.

DRIP, DRIP, DRIP

The two months that followed were brutal.

Having to move house in order to deal with the continual police visits, without disturbing our neighbours, was a harsh pill to swallow. I loved the Tudor. It was a mansion that had been converted into several townhouses and functioned like a private estate. It was beautiful and glorious, but it just wasn't fair on our rather elderly neighbours to put them through such volatility. We had become the family that no-one wanted to live in close proximity to, and so we made sure that the new house was detached.

It was a beautiful double-story Edwardian, in one of the wealthiest suburbs of Melbourne, Australia. I don't say this to boast. I say this to confirm what I have learned along the way. It doesn't matter how much money you earn, how beautiful a house you live in, and how fancy the cars are that you drive, behind every fortified wall, no matter how tall, are individual hearts struggling with disappointment, heartache, loneliness, a lack of identity and purpose. All of which lead to a desperate need to silence their constant dripping.

Drip. Drip. Drip.

Relationships find themselves in the middle of tectonic plates about to shift. Mental health gives way, and in seeps depression, anxiety, or suicidal thoughts and then before long, the emergence of 'acting out of the norm' begins to take shape. In severe cases, we see domestic violence, abuse, adultery, murder, rape. For others it goes as far as addictions such as alcohol, drugs, gambling, or pornography. Whatever choices are made, the objective is to numb the pain.

For my Björn, drugs allowed him to escape his diagnosis, his loneliness, and his troubled mind. The gang welcomed him in and made him feel like he belonged.

The burden of his continual disappearing acts for days on end, with no communication weighed heavy. Then the unexpected squeak of the gate at three o'clock in the morning would have me wake, saturated in fear.

The distant hum of voices, the closing of car doors led to penetrating thoughts coursing through my mind. Who was he with? Why were they parked outside our home? The turning of the key in the front-door, the sound of the shower, and the raiding of the fridge all carried with it an eeriness that I couldn't shake.

By morning, though he looked like death-warmed-up, he'd rustle up breakfast and flick on the kettle, as if nothing had happened. He'd be chatty, cracking jokes and certainly coming across like he'd sorted himself out and was on the up and up.

Sandro would ruffle the boy's hair, kiss me on the cheek, and as he headed out, he'd turn and signal for me to call him, whilst giving me the reassuring thumbs up that everything would fine. The three of us would sit down together over the freshly prepared breakfast with all the trimmings. I wouldn't be able to eat, and I couldn't speak either.

Some days, just a simple question would result in him flaring up from nought to hundred into a fit of uncontrollable rage, that would leave me cowering in fear for what he might do. Neither Ramon nor I could handle repeats of such scenes, and so we continued to suffer in silence whilst portraying normalcy.

Björn would then offer to do the dishes, whilst Ramon headed out the door for work, and I stepped into my office for my day of coaching appointments. Afterall, we couldn't just stop because of what was unravelling, but it certainly wasn't easy trying to continue with living life either.

Half-way through my first meeting of the day, I'd hear the dreaded sound of the front-door clicking, and I'd watch through the window as my Björn disappeared down the garden path, without even a goodbye.

My heart would plummet, and I'd have to fight to stay focussed on my meeting at hand. The squeak of the gate once more. The distant hum of voices, the closing of car doors. And he'd be gone.

This continuation of comings and goings, the inability to eat or sleep, fear, dread, outburst of tears, glimpses of my Ramon listening in on heated conversations, the constant knocking on our front-door with police all too familiar with our names. 'Where is he Mrs Tranquim?' they would ask. Fatigued I would respond, 'You know the answer to this. I haven't a clue where he is.'

We had all reached breaking point. Our son's drug-fuelled behaviour had become more and more erratic, to the point, he was now a danger to us all. We had no choice; we had to make the call.

The next time he snuck in at three o'clock in the morning, Sandro woke and placed his hand on my weary head. 'Settle your heart Babe,' he said, 'I'm on it.'

Together as a family we sat at our dining room table, with cups of tea in hand. Björn sat opposite his dad, fidgeting to get out. Ramon and I sat with our heads bowed as Sandro led the charge. Looking at Björn, he leant over and with compassion in his voice, made very clear our love and commitment towards him. He reassured him that if at any point he needed us, he could always reach out, and no matter what, we would be there for him.

Sandro then sat upright, and in a more serious stance, explained that we as parents not only had a duty of care towards him, but towards his brother, our Ramon also. I could see Ramon's eyes light up in that moment. It was so special to hear Sandro stand up for him in this way.

Pointing in my direction, Sandro went on that part of his duty as my husband is to take care of my wellbeing. Our lives had been in turmoil for long enough, and we just couldn't go on as things were.

Then, without warning, Sandro's tone shifted gears as he laid it all out on the line.

Björn could no longer have the best of both worlds. He had to choose one or the other. He either had to admit that he had a drug problem and wanted help, in which case, we would do everything in our power to get him the help that he needed. Or, if wanted to choose a life of drugs and gangs, he would have to leave. But it wasn't going to continue under our roof.

At that, Björn blew.

'I don't have a drug problem!' he exclaimed as he leapt to his feet with such force, spilling his tea all over the dining room table. I rushed to the kitchen to grab a dishcloth, whilst he stormed to his room to pack his bags. I could hear Sandro reassuring Ramon that this needed to happen. Deep down, I knew it too, but oh my heart was broken. Without a word, I watched my boy slam the door behind him as he left.

Scathing text messages from him started hitting my phone, which led to Ramon blocking Björn's number altogether. I felt broken beyond repair, like my heart had been shattered into a million pieces and could never be put back together. I lay on my bed in a foetal position and wept. A heaviness filled my home that day.

REPENTANCE UNLOCKS THE DOOR

I need you to understand that you are, to the future generations, a generation of the past. Whilst you know the authority you carry to break the sins and curses of *past* generations in your bloodline, I want to challenge you with this question, "Why not break the sins and curses of your *current* generation also?" We shouldn't leave the clean-up of our generation to the generations of the future.

I knew that my son's drug addiction was directly linked to his diagnosis. A hereditary illness, that to us as children of God, we grew to understand was in fact a generational curse on our family's bloodline, as a direct result of generational sin passed down.

These generational sins have since been repented of before God. Despite not knowing what they were name-for-name, our God is all knowing and all powerful. The curses attached to those sins have now been broken through the act of repentance, and by our appropriation of Jesus's blood poured out over our bloodline.

Unfortunately for some, the word 'repentance' has a very negative connotation. The image of a guilt-ridden human approaching an angry and judgemental God gives off an 'I'd rather be anywhere else' kind of vibe. But this image is a lie. God in Heaven is not angry and just waiting to strike you down. He's a loving and merciful God, who longs for a deep connection with you. Romans 8:38-39 says it beautifully.

> 'And I am convinced that nothing can ever separate us from
> God's love. Neither death nor life, neither angels nor demons,
> neither our fears for today nor our worries about tomorrow—
> not even the powers of hell can separate us from God's love. No
> power in the sky above or in the earth below—indeed, nothing
> in all creation will ever be able to separate us from the love of
> God that is revealed in Christ Jesus our Lord.'

Here's the image that I have in my mind when I come before God, in a posture of repentance. I picture the cross. I'm taken back to the day when my Lord Jesus gave His life for me. He paid the ransom for my sin with His life, to set me free. I therefore don't need to live under the curse of sin, and this not only applies to me, but it also applies to you.

So, as I begin to pray out aloud, I imagine myself lifting off from my shoulders whatever burden it is that I've been carrying and placing that burden at the foot of the cross. I not only feel a physical letting go; I feel it mentally and emotionally also. Matthew 18:18 (NET Translation) confirms this release:

> "I tell you the truth, whatever you bind on earth will have
> been bound in heaven, and whatever you release on earth will
> have been released in heaven."

Repentance is an act of faith that releases the power of forgiveness. This release impacts your whole being.

This kind of repentance is like the little kid who's been found out. In fact, I'm reminded of one particular scenario from when I was a little girl. I was standing on a chair in the pantry, nicking the hundreds and thousands from my mama's stash of baking goodies, when she walked in, stood at the entrance and without warning, bellowed in my direction, almost sending me crashing to the ground, 'What on earth are you doing young lady?'

Oh my gosh, I awkwardly caught my balance as I contemplated my next move. I couldn't just shove the next handful in my mouth, or I'd be well and truly done. Turning in her direction with fear and trepidation, there was no doubt by the evidence sprawled across my chops, that I was guilty. However, the apology wasn't because I was truly sorry for diving into the sugary lushness of hundreds and thousands, it was more so for being caught. You know exactly what I mean. That rather agitated and slightly arrogant blurt-out of the word, 'Sorry.'

True repentance is done from a posture of humility. It's got nothing to do with being caught, and everything to do with being remorseful for one's actions. Whether your own, or that of another. In the case of repenting for generational sin, Sandro and I came before God in humility and with remorse for the actions of our previous generations.

When a curse is broken, sometimes it's immediate. Other times, there is an outworking that needs to take place within the person who was living under the curse, prior to repentance.

A curse impacts people differently, but it impacts everyone in what I call **The Six Pillars of a Human Life**. Namely: -

1. Spiritual Pillar
2. Mental Pillar
3. Emotional Pillar
4. Physical Pillar
5. Relational Pillar
6. Financial Pillar

All six pillars are required in order to live and function. The first three are *inward* pillars. The last three are *outward*.

You may be wondering why the physical pillar is only listed at number four. Well, everything that happens inwardly affects us outwardly.

Allow me to give you a birds-eye-view example of how the impact of a curse affects all six pillars.

Picture yourself at ten years of age in the playground at school. The class bully with their little gang is heading straight in your direction and you feel your body clam up. Without warning, they shove you to the ground and yell at the top of their lungs, 'You are the weakest person in the entire school.' This scene relates to your spiritual pillar, and I will explain more later.

On the spot, a seed is planted within your mind. Now we've moved on to your mental pillar. Their words smash you to the core. All you can think about for the rest of the day is how weak you are. Their one statement takes root within your heart, and the seed begins to germinate from a thought, into a belief. You then start to self-declare, 'I am weak.' And you find yourself repeating this line all the way home.

By the time you get in the door, you are a mess. The impact has now hit your emotional pillar. You storm through the house, dump your lunchbox in the kitchen and then run upstairs to your room where you crash on your bed and sob into your pillow. You don't want to come down for dinner, but you do. Your eyes are blood-shot, and your family can see that something is wrong.

The impact on your emotions now starts to outwork in your physical behaviour. This is your physical pillar. You are moody, you're sad. Your response to questions about your day is short and snappy. You end up yelling at your sibling, you kick the dog, and you don't even join the family for your favourite show after. The physical impact over time is seen in the way that you continue to carry yourself. You're walking with your head down, you avoid eye contact, you might even begin to find yourself sitting further and further back in group settings, like the classroom, or on the field.

This then has a knock-on-effect on your relationships. This is your relational pillar. Walls are erected because you're guarded. Afterall, you don't want to allow yourself to be hurt again. Your friends struggle to connect with you and before long, they start dropping like flies, because they can't cope with your outbursts anymore. You then find yourself isolated and alone.

The impact on your financial pillar could be a drastic change in spend. At ten years of age, your pocket money is no longer going into savings for that new toy you've had your eye on. Instead, you're straight down to the corner shop shovelling in chocolate, crisps and pies to try and appease the ache.

Can you see the cycle? Oh, it's my prayer that as you read this book, you come into an awareness and understanding of what's happening around you, like never before. Let's dive deeper.

INWARD PILLARS

As much as we are physical beings, we are spiritual beings first. I have come to learn that everything that happens in life is a direct result of what is happening in the spiritual realm around us. This is emphasised in the following scripture:

Ephesians 6:12 says,

> *'For we do not wrestle against flesh and blood, but against principalities, against power, against the rules of darkness of this age, against spiritual hosts of wickedness in the heavenly places.'*

When we don't understand this principle, we don't clearly see the battle that takes place around us in the spiritual realm. This isn't about the bully charging in your direction. This is about Satan with his cohorts, wanting to take you out, and he will do anything to sabotage your future.

John 10:10 says,

> 'The thief does not come except to steal, and to kill, and to destroy. I (Jesus) have come that they may have life, and that they may have it more abundantly.'

Allow me to elaborate further by continuing with our family's journey. For my son Björn, aside from the physical impact of the hereditary disease, it all began at a spiritual level with the enemy whispering into his ear not long after his diagnosis.

Whispers like, 'You're going to die, and there's nothing you can do about it.'

Satan's lies were like seeds in Björn's mind. His thoughts began to run wild, as he formed images in his mind of what he thought was going to happen to him.

Before long, those seeds began to germinate, and the lies went from a thought to a belief. This then led to a mental and emotional spiralling.

Anxiety took a hold. The whispering lies continued.

'Your parents are too busy coming to terms with the upending of their lives, the continual back and forth for hospital appointments, packing up and relocating to America. They don't have time to listen to your little fears about your impending death.'

Satan knew that if Björn were to speak out, we as a family would rally around him, we would come against the schemes of the enemy, we would not allow Björn to go down the rabbit hole of mental and emotional demise, and we would walk him through the process of taking his thoughts captive, until he was completely free of those lies.

2 Corinthians 10:3-5 in the Amplified Bible puts it like this:

> *For though we walk in the flesh (as mortal men), we are not carrying on our (spiritual) warfare according to the flesh and using the weapons of man. The weapons of our warfare are not physical (weapons of flesh and blood). Our weapons are divinely powerful for the destruction of fortresses. We are destroying sophisticated arguments and every exalted and proud thing that sets itself up against the (true) knowledge of God, and we are taking every thought and purpose captive to the obedience of Christ.*

Instead, Satan had silenced my boy, and the anxiety escalated.

The volume of the voices in his little head were only amplified by concerned faces of family and friends.

Over time, the weight of the anxiety that had taken a hold of his heart turned into depression. An underlying sadness consumed him, so he faked laughter in the hope that no one would notice.

A desperate need to silence the voices, to be able to sleep without the grip of fear, led to thoughts of suicide.

The anxiety and depression were then compounded by not only suicidal thoughts, but feelings of guilt and shame at the prospect of how his suicide would impact his family.

'I couldn't do that to them.' He surmised.

And now there's no escape from his inner turmoil.

Satan was doing everything in his power to take my Björn out. But he knew his whispers of anxiety, depression and suicide weren't working, and so he had to change tactic. The enemy then looked for a gateway in.

OUTWARD PILLARS

Björn is lured into the lifestyle of a budding chef. He's gleaning from the generations before him, who smoke weed in the alleyways to come off their adrenaline high from the night, and to numb their own internal war, was how it was done. You're now witnessing the physical impact of Björn's mental and emotional state coupled with the influences around him. A perfect storm if you will.

Before long, Björn began to realise that the weed gave him a semblance of relief from the incessant dripping within his inner pillars. A euphoric moment that allowed him to erase the illness altogether. To numb the anxiety, depression and suicidal thoughts leaving him with a counterfeit of happiness, relaxation, and creativity like he'd not experienced in years. Relationally he's moving closer and closer to these toxic people, whilst being pulled further and further away from his family and church connections who really love him. No doubt the paper-trail of his bank statements reflected accordingly.

PAUSE AND PONDER

Take some time to evaluate where you are at right now in relation to the six pillars of your own life.

Ask yourself, 'What sins and/or curses am I bound by in my generation, that future generations will be impacted by, if I don't deal with them now?'

Then, go into a time of prayer. Here's an example of what you could say:

'Holy Spirit, thank You for Your presence. Thank You that You are my helper. Jesus, I love you and I acknowledge You as my Lord and Saviour. Thank You for giving me access to Father God.

Father, thank You for Your love for me. Thank You for sending Your Son to die on Calvary. Thank You that You want the best for me and my loved ones.

Reveal to me through the power of Holy Spirit exactly what needs to be brought to the forefront, so that I can lay these matters at the foot of the cross and receive Your healing, restoration and deliverance.

In Jesus name, Amen.'

Reflect on each pillar in your life one at a time, and jot down your findings.

1. Spiritual Pillar. What situations have occurred in my life that were actually schemes of Satan to take out my walk with God?
2. Mental Pillar. How did those schemes impact me mentally?
3. Emotional Pillar. How did those schemes impact me emotionally?
4. Physical Pillar. What's been the physical impact/outworking of those schemes in my life?
5. Relational Pillar. How did those schemes impact my relationships with my loved ones?
6. Financial Pillar. What was the knock-on-effect in my finances?

Don't rush this process.

The Lord may bring revelation in a heartbeat, but He may do it over a period of time. Submit to the process, be kind to yourself and your loved ones in the midst of it, because some of what He shows you may be a little uncomfortable to come to terms with. But know this. Your healing and freedom are at hand.

CHAPTER 8

WARZONE

THE PRODIGAL SON

I remember looking at my face in the mirror the next day. It was pale and drawn. The effects of the last few years had well and truly taken their toll. And now my boy, who was in total denial of his addiction, had stormed out the door without a trace. I lent on the bathroom sink as tears began to fall, and I softly cried out to Jesus, 'I just don't have the courage to face this.'

My hair appointment couldn't have come at a better time. I walked into the salon later that day, and my beautiful hairdresser Jordan looked at me as if to say, 'What on earth has happened?' He sat me down and offered me a comforting cup of tea. For the first time in weeks, I felt like I could breathe.

'And what are we doing today?' he asked with a smirk on his face and a glint of cheek in his eyes, whilst squeezing my shoulders. He didn't know anything about what had transpired since seeing him for my previous appointment, but he didn't have to. He knew the second he saw me that I was not okay.

'Shave it.' I announced.

Jordan is certainly not one to shy away from a radical change in style. He was all in, and I loved him for it. In fact, that was the beginning of the hairstyle I carry to this day. My reasoning, I needed to be able to look at myself in the mirror and see a bad-ass warrior staring back at me, who wasn't afraid of what was to come.

What did come however, was brutal. I'm not going to go into the ins and outs, but I will say, it was worse than watching my son undergo his treatment just three years prior. I will, however, share one particular scene that occurred several months after my hair salon visit to Jordan.

Sandro and I were battle-worn. We had never known such intensity from one day to the next. It was like living on a knifes-edge, and we woke one Sunday morning, struggling to put one foot in front of the other. We knew we needed to get ourselves to church, and so we pushed.

Fatigued and flailing, we walked through the church doors, where we were welcomed by friends who had loved and supported us, and then slumped into our seats as we waited for the service to begin. The worship was stunning and felt like a summers rain washing over us. After we got home, Sandro went to put the kettle on, and I walked into our lounge, stood at my piano, and gazed over my quaint English garden, when suddenly the hair on the back of my neck stood to attention.

There on our little lover's bench, surrounded by roses lay my Björn. I must have physically reacted because Sandro came running in asking if I was okay. He looked in the direction of where I was staring, and I knew he too was taken aback. By this point our boy had been living on the streets. He was heavily involved with a gang and police calls and visits were a regular theme. And to be blunt, our family was broken.

Without a word, Sandro softly headed out the door and gently approached our boy. I watched as he lovingly spoke with him, and I could tell by his body language what he was saying. 'Why are you choosing this lifestyle when you have a family who loves you and a home to shelter you?' Oh, how my heart ached. Sandro managed to convince him to come inside. I remained in the lounge, watching from afar, as they walked towards the front door. He went straight upstairs to shower and then caught up on some much-needed sleep.

Sandro and I both knew that we had to attend the evening service at church that night. We needed to be in the presence of our God, and in the company of our faith-filled friends. Ramon was home and said he would keep a listen out in case Björn woke up.

For the second time that day, we slumped into our seats as we waited for the service to begin, when the live feed from our parent campus connected earlier than usual. The senior pastor was talking to his congregation, my mind was preoccupied, and flitted in and out when out of nowhere, the atmosphere changed. I looked up at the screen and watched as the senior pastor looked straight into the camera and said with authority and conviction, 'I don't know why, and I don't know who's watching this, but I just feel we need to pray for the return of the prodigal sons right now.'

I couldn't believe what I had just heard. Immediately I felt a rush of emotion well up from my gut. Sandro and I both turned to each other in complete shock. Images of our boy lying on our garden bench earlier in the day came flooding back. Sandro standing outside challenging him on his lifestyle choices, reminding him of his family who loved him more than he would ever realise.

The auditorium was full by this point, the worship team were preparing to start the service, and then the senior pastor went on to say, 'Which ever campus you are at right now, if you have a prodigal son in your family, I want you to stand to your feet.' Sandro and I stood to attention without giving it a second thought or even signalling to one another of each other's intent. We both knew this moment was for us.

Sandro wrapped his arm around me, and I wept. My mama's heart was broken for my boy. Before long, all of our treasured friends were rallied around us. The pastor prayed. He called all the prodigal sons home. Hope filled my heart once more, and even though our reality looked impossible to fix, I knew in my heart that God was on His throne.

By the time we got home, our Björn had left.

I sat at the bottom of his bed and cried.

A KNOCK AT THE DOOR

Three days later, there was a knock at the door.

I froze.

There is nothing worse than the sound of a knock on your door when you have a young adult son denying their drug addiction, whilst choosing a lifestyle that is dangerous in and of itself, without the compounded dimension of a life-threatening disease. Every door knock throughout the last few months sent my mind into turmoil.

The cycle was simple but brutal.

I'd hear the door, and immense heat would run through my body. My heart would begin to race, my forehead clammy with sweat, and I'd begin to feel faint. Clinging to the banister I'd make my way slowly downstairs, hoping I wouldn't collapse. I'd be desperately praying that it wasn't the police coming to report that they'd found a body.

'Oh God, give me strength.' I'd pray.

Pausing at the front door, I'd have to consciously slow my breathing. I'd close my eyes and press my fingers against each thumb imagining the slow rhythm of a metronome in an attempt to slow my breathing. I'd then inhale deeply before letting out one long exhale as I unlocked the latch.

On this day, I did all of the above, and when I opened the door, my body leapt backward in horror at the emaciated figure standing before me.

It was my precious Björn.

Oh, my boy.

For the first time since holding this baby in my arms, even after everything he went through in hospital, I was petrified for his life. His weak frame wouldn't be able to continue this lifestyle for much longer.

He evidently wasn't taking his medication, he looked like he hadn't eaten in weeks, he was dehydrated and drawn. He literally looked like a skeleton. He didn't have the strength to react to my shock. I quickly composed myself, warmly smiled and welcomed him in, offering him a cup of tea as I held back any outward expression of my wrenching heart.

He sat opposite me at the dining room table, with his head hung low. His scrawny hands hugging his mug.

'And how's my boy doing?' I gently asked, holding back the tears.

His eyes wearily looked up at mine.

'Not good mom. Not good.'

It was as if the lights had gone out. As much as I just wanted to wrap my arms around him, hold him tight and tell him that everything was going to be okay and we were going to get him all the help he needed, I knew it would be futile.

We had been around this mountain many times before. I had to remain strong. My *boy* had to admit that he needed help, and he had to *want* that help for himself. All I could do was pray and wait for that moment to come.

He ate, showered, and slept. I texted Sandro soon after Björn arrived, to let him know that he was visiting. Sandro reassured me that he was on his way and wouldn't be long. I had several coaching clients booked in the calendar from weeks prior that I needed to tend to, so that evening Sandro took Björn out for a drive.

To my surprise, when he arrived back later that evening, he returned with Björn. I was laying on the sofa in the lounge, mentally and emotionally depleted. I couldn't go on like this. Something had to change, but I didn't know how that looked.

Sandro went upstairs to shower, when Björn came and sat opposite me. He looked a little more human than he had when I opened the door to him earlier. I didn't have the strength to get up and so stayed where I was. There was an awkwardness to the silence, and I'm sure I dipped out in sleep for a moment or two.

I knew the drill, as we'd done this several times over the last few months. Eventually I asked, 'Where would you like dad to drop you tonight?' My eyes remained shut. Part exhaustion, and part denial. I didn't want to hear the words, 'Oh, just drop me at Flinders Street Station.' Or 'Can you drop me at my mates in Glen Iris?'

I was done.

His reply sent goosebumps shooting through my body.

'I can't do this anymore mom.'

There was a seriousness to his tone.

I opened my eyes to his silhouette in front of me, as the crackle of the fire behind him only emphasised his hunched-up form. The room seemed darker, as if I'd slept for ages.

'What did you say?' I asked, hoping I hadn't heard wrong.

'I can't do this anymore mom. I know I have a drug problem; I'm in trouble and I need help.'

At that, I sat upright just as Sandro walked in, with curiosity on his brow, as to what was being discussed.

I asked Björn to repeat what he had just said to me so Sandro could hear it with his own ears. He did. Sandro was rubbing moisturiser into his hands and when Björn was done, he very matter of fact replied to his boy, 'We will help you, but you will need to ring the rehab centre tomorrow for yourself,' to which Björn agreed. We allowed Björn to sleep in his own bed that night, on the proviso that he would remain at home, and would not contact any of his people. He agreed to that also.

Before we all went to bed, I knocked on Ramon's door and spent some time with him, sharing what had happened earlier in the evening. He was pleased to hear that Björn was potentially coming to his senses, and I knew he would be there to support us as we navigated the days ahead. I can't imagine how hard all of this would have been for Ramon. His whole life had been turned upside down also. All he could do was watch and wait from the sidelines. Oh, but the comfort he brought his mama's heart. I don't think he will ever fully realise.

As much as my body so desperately needed sleep, I just couldn't.

I was a mama on the night watch, and I was not about to let my son out of my sight. My hearing had sharpened over the last several months. Every little move, every cough, every toilet-stop, every light switch, every car driving by, every creek of the gate, every turning of keys and closing of doors, nothing went unnoticed.

I felt myself exhale in relief at the sound of birds awakening, as first light dawned. The last few months had been building to this very moment, and I knew there was a weightiness to the days ahead. As I sat on the edge of my bed enjoying a moment's kiss from the morning sun, I knew deep down that my boy's life hung in the balance.

GET HIM OUT

When I think back now, I know it was the Holy Spirit who dropped into my heart the words, 'You need to get Björn out of town.' It was as clear as the day breaking before me. All I knew was we had to get Björn out of Melbourne before the weekend hit. It was only years later that I learned the biggest drug-fuelled nights of the week are Fridays and Saturdays.

As I sat on my bed that Thursday morning, I texted friends who lived on a farm about three hours out of the city. I didn't go into detail, but I asked if we could find refuge at theirs for a few nights. They replied with an instant yes.

The house was still. Sandro made me a cup of tea and I shared with him that as soon as Björn was accepted into rehab we needed to get him out of Melbourne. He reassured me that he and Ramon would not be going in to work that day, and that we as a family would get through the next few days together.

Throughout the course of the previous several months I had been on the phone to rehabilitation centres across Australia, so that when my boy came to his senses, we would know our next step. Of all the calls I had made, there was only one rehabilitation centre that I found whose primary objective is to **rid** individuals of addiction. All the rest only helped to **manage** it. We were not interested in our Björn *managing* his addiction when our Heavenly Father promises us in Ephesians 3:20 that He is able to do exceedingly abundantly above all that we ask or think. We were not willing to settle, we were expecting *total* healing and freedom for him.

As soon as Björn woke up and had a bite to eat, he went and sat outside on the very same bench that he had slept on just a few days prior. There, he made the call to the rehab centre. I prayed and cried as I watched him from my lounge room. 'Oh Lord, please let them have a place for him.'

The whole day felt like we were waiting. It was several hours later when Björn received the call from the rehab centre to say that they had one place available, and that it was his if he wanted it. He immediately responded with a 'Yes!' And they advised that he needed to report to their centre in Sydney first thing the next Tuesday morning, and he had to have been clean of drugs for a minimum of forty-eight hours.

I knew we were in for a battle.

It was special sitting down to dinner as a family for the first time in months that night. But I had a nervousness within me that I just couldn't shake. We had a drug addicted son, caught up in a gang that you don't just walk away from, with five full days in front of us. I knew I wouldn't be sleeping that night either. But I also had this growing urgency within me, to get our boy out of Melbourne.

It was a long night and as dawn broke, I frantically began to pack. Sandro woke Ramon and Björn and explained that we would be leaving Melbourne that afternoon, in order to start the road trip to Sydney. Ramon agreed to help us prepare and would look after the house while we were away.

Björn was *irate* because he wanted one last evening with his mates. I can only describe my response as a mama bear riling up within me, because I knew we could not allow this to happen. A war broke out between us which I knew was spiritual. As it says in scripture in Ephesians 6:12 (NKJV),

For we wrestle not against flesh and blood, but against principalities, against powers, against the rules of the darkness of this world, against spiritual wickedness in high places.

This war that broke out between us was spiritual but the manifestation of that war in the physical realm, was Björn not wanting to leave Melbourne without saying goodbye to his mates. I was not about to allow him any further time with the very people who were destroying his life.

I need you to take stock of the spiritual component at play here, which I will elaborate on, later in the chapter.

In the end, Sandro and I both knew we had to reach a negotiation or a peace treaty (if you want to remain within the analogy of war), or Björn would leave regardless. I am fully convinced that had Björn gone that night, any alcohol or drugs would have resulted in his body giving way and the dreaded scene of police coming to my door to say they had found a body would have come true.

After Sandro and I spoke, the four of us sat together, where we told Björn that we would shout pizza, and he could invite all of his drug and gang members to our house, so he could say goodbye within the safe confines of our presence. They would have a window to meet. The time stamp was given, and then we would be leaving Melbourne.

I think about this now and I'm like, 'What on earth were you thinking??' But it worked. Our boy was happy with the arrangement, and so he reached out to all of his contacts, and we nervously waited.

No one showed up.

Sandro, Ramon and I began loading the car, but our Björn didn't want to go. I still remember storming heaven with my prayers. In the end, Ramon literally grabbed Björn's hand, led him to the car, strapped him in and closed the door. He hugged me and told me that Björn was going to be just fine and that he'd have a cup of tea waiting on our arrival back home in a few days' time.

With that, Sandro, Björn and I left.

THE WHEELS FELL OFF

The days that followed were scarier than one can imagine. Our boy had already been fiending for drugs from the time he came knocking on our door, just three days prior. His addiction was worse than we realised, and he was experiencing full-blown withdrawal. We somehow had to make the three-hour drive to our friend's farm with him being agitated, anxious and paranoid. Then, we still had to lay-low for three days before making our way to Sydney.

It was three nights of hell for this mama and papa, as we listened to him waking in the night, talking under his breath, rummaging around as if looking for something. The haunting sounds of him opening and closing the front door. All of this, with the constant reminder in the back of our minds that he had to be clean for a minimum of forty-eight hours in order to be accepted into rehab. I praise God for our friends whose farm was so large, that even if he had tried to run, there was no-where for him to run to.

We arrived in the Blue Mountains of Sydney and woke that Tuesday morning with nerves of knots. Sleep-deprived and anxious, none of us could eat, so we quietly and swiftly packed our bags and made our way to the rehab centre.

Turning off the main road, we headed down a magnificent treelined entrance. Flashbacks of the treelined entrance leading to my piano lessons as a little girl came flooding back. Only this time, it was thirty-seven years later, and the destination was a drug and alcohol rehabilitation centre that was birthed in the very same year that my husband Sandro was born.

The drop-off was abrupt.

I don't know if I imagined us all having a celebratory barbeque where we'd meet all the lads and exchange stories, but that certainly didn't happen. We arrived at the reception and completed paperwork while Björn was taken through for his bag-search and drug and alcohol test. When everything came back clear, we were given a few minutes to say goodbye.

That was it.

Before we knew it, Sandro and I were back in the car for the nine-and-a-half-hour journey home to Melbourne.

As I leant my head on the passenger window, gazing out at the Australian bushlands around me, I felt a sense of relief for the first time in years. My boy was finally safe. He was going to get the care and attention that he so desperately needed, and his mama could now breathe. Closing my eyes the tears began to stream.

As the long drive home continued, my emotions slipped from relief into what I can only describe as a deep unravelling. It was as if I had let my guard down for the first time in years. I had been holding it all in, and not just from the events of the last few months, but from the time Björn was first diagnosed some five years prior.

When we eventually pulled up outside our double-story quaint red-brick home, I walked in, hugged my Ramon tight, quietly drank his promised cup of tea, and then headed straight to bed. I don't think I've ever slept so much as I did in the three days that followed.

Sandro drew the curtains back and came and sat on the bed, greeting me with a fresh cup of tea. He propped up my pillows, and after a few moments went on to tell me that he had booked a doctor's appointment for me, and that I needed to get myself ready. I didn't argue. That in itself was evidence that I knew I was not okay.

The appointment was a blur. I vaguely remember answering a questionnaire and faintly hearing garbled talk between the doctor and Sandro, as I ticked boxes.

I waited as the doctor reviewed my answers. He scribbled notes and waited some more. What felt like hours later, he eventually looked up and officially diagnosed me with Chronic PTSD, Anxiety and Depression. My head was down. I had nothing. No reaction, no response, no thought, nothing.

I could hear the doctor's gentle voice as he spoke *of* me in the third person to Sandro, as if I wasn't in the room. He was right. I don't know where I was, but I certainly wasn't in the room.

He empathetically explained to Sandro that he was putting me on a mental health care plan, and that I needed to attended weekly appointments with a psychologist, for a minimum of six months. He prescribed antibiotics and then requested a follow-up appointment for a month's time.

I know I have used these exact words in the book already, but it describes just how I felt in the days that followed.

I felt broken beyond repair. It was like my heart had been shattered into a million pieces and could never be put back together again.

Emotionally, I was grieving the loss of my son, yet I wrestled with guilt and shame for grieving, because it wasn't like he was dead. He was very much alive and was getting the help he needed. I felt bad for being so absent towards my eldest son. Even as I write this book there have been moments in the writing process where I've asked Sandro, 'Where was Ramon when all of this was happening?'

Ramon was a quiet comfort throughout every ordeal, and a ferocious protector when he needed to be. But he also deserved the love and attention of his mama that I just couldn't give him. Mentally I was trapped in the past, as scenes continued to replay over and over in my mind again. In the depths of despair, I couldn't figure my way out of my mental maze, and all sense of purpose was gone. For the past five years I had poured into the tending and caring of a single individual who was now no longer with me. How do I move on from here? How do I get back up, dust off the dirt and keep on going, just like I so boldly advised readers of my previous book?

Physically, my body was shot. My hands were constantly shaking, stepping one foot in front of the other was laboursome, and I could have quite happily slept my life away.

Yet while my physical, mental, and emotional being were in the worst condition it had ever been in my entire life, my spirit was strong.

'Where was God in the midst of all of this?' You may ask.

Oh, He was right there. I felt His presence every step of the way. In fact, I remember this one particular day, right in the middle of this six-month period of my very own rehabilitation, where I found myself at home, alone. Both Sandro and Ramon were out, and the deafening silence around me beckoned me out of bed and led me to my piano.

It had remained untouched for some time. Its majestic curves highlighted by the glow of the afternoon's glistening sun. Bouncing reflections of branches and leaves, I gazed out of the window at the comforting sound and sight of birds fluttering, chirping and nesting, reminding me that life must go on.

I sat.

I slowly opened the lid, placed my fingers on the ivories, closed my eyes and took a deep inhale. A new melody washed over me, and I exhaled. I could hear a sound from heaven. Before I knew it, I found myself singing a refrain that I had written over twelve years prior, while still a worship leader in London. I began singing over and over,

> *'I'm falling in love with You.*
> *I'm falling in love with You. I*
> *'m falling in love, I'm falling in love,*
> *I'm falling in love with You*
> *Over and over again.'*

The whole day passed, and I didn't leave my piano. The presence of God was so tangible, and I knew in the silence and my aloneness, that He was doing a deep healing work within me. His loving embrace was anchoring me even though I felt like I had come to the end of myself. He began to release a new sound threaded with poetry and it was in this moment that I wrote the song, 'Your Love.'

It was in my own unravelling that I began to see what was really happening around me. Nothing of what we had been through as a family over the years was about the physical realm. Sure, it all took place in the physical, but it was all as a result of what was happening in the spirit realm.

Earlier I asked that you to take stock of the spiritual component at play, on the day that we were due to get Björn out of town.

He was irate about seeing his friends one last time, and we fought against it. I knew in that moment that what we were experiencing in the physical realm, was a manifestation of what was happening in the spirit realm. There was a spiritual war taking place for his soul. I am now going to elaborate further, and so take a deep breath in, because this is going to be a mind-bending revelation for you. I believe that as you awaken to this truth, you are going to be able to apply the principles and step into healing, restoration and freedom in your own life. But first, allow the melody and lyrics of 'Your Love wash over you.

Scan Code for Your Love

SPIRIT AND EARTH REALM

The reality I was waking up to is that there is a spiritual battle taking place for the souls of humanity. God in heaven is longing for His children to acknowledge Him through His Son Jesus, so that the relationship between God and man is restored. Meanwhile, Satan, the banished angel from heaven who went by the name of lucifer, prowls around like a roaring lion, seeking whom he can devour. His primary objective is to kill, steal and destroy as echoed in John 10:10 and he will use any means by which to succeed.

What happens in the spirit realm manifests in the earth realm, and the extent of this manifestation includes sins, and their curses passed down from generation to generation. Allow me to explain.

The hereditary blood disorder was a generational curse passed down from previous generations in our bloodline. It killed my brother, and now my son was a victim of its clutches. While we don't know why this curse found it's place in our bloodline, nor do we know the details of any sin that may have taken place in previous generations that led to this curse moving in, we were certainly a generation that saw it for what it was and knew the authority we carried in Jesus.

When it comes to generational sin and curses, we hold the authority in Jesus's Name to break those sins and curses, not only over our current generation, but over future generations to come.

Through prayer and intercession, we came before God and asked that He break the curse of sickness over our son. Our prayers also included all our future generations until the return of Jesus. We prayed in faith believing that Jesus's cleansing blood has healed our bloodline of this curse, and we now live in the freedom of the finished work of the cross. Has Björn been completely healed? Yes, we believe so. The manifestation of his complete healing is still a process. He still needs doctors' visits and ongoing tests, but he is not living as a victim any longer. He's living from a place of victory, because of what he believes and Who he believes in.

Now let's look at how *new* curses are formed in the current generation. Please understand that curses don't always stem from an outward act of sin. Sometimes curses stem from the soft, subtle whispers of Satan.

What I'm about to say is mind-bending revelation to me, even as I write it.

Generational sin and curses, seed in the spirit realm and manifest in the physical realm through the **Six Pillars of a Human Life** that I covered in Chapter Seven.

In other words, what is seeded in the spirit realm can manifest physically, mentally, emotionally, spiritually, relationally, and financially.

I'm going to give you a birds-eye view of how new curses are formed in our current generation, by using Björn's story as an example.

Lies from Satan had infiltrated Björn's mind when he was first diagnosed through whispers like, 'You will never get better. In fact, you will die an early death. Can you imagine how painful that process will be? No one will be able to do anything about it. You are doomed. You will never achieve what you thought you would as a little boy. You'll never see your friends again. You'll never fall in love, get married or have children of your own.'

Those lies stemmed in the spirit realm and manifested in the physical realm through soft whispers in Björn's ear. The moment he *believed* those lies was the moment they became active curses to him. In other words, by believing the lies, he gave them legal right to torment him. Oh, and the lies moved in.

A believed lie becomes a curse.

By the time we witness what's going on around us in the physical realm, there's already been a whole process prior that has taken place in the spirit realm.

The manifestation of these curses in Björn's case, led him on a mental and emotional downward spiral, that resulted in depression, anxiety, and suicidal thoughts. In a desperate attempt to numb the anguish of his soul, he started taking physical steps which ultimately led him to his drug and alcohol addiction. The spiral deepened as he needed to find ways to fuel his habit and so got sucked into the gang culture and started doing things he never used to, and so the vicious cycle continued. His relationships with his family and church friends dissipated, he moved away from God entirely and became more and more drawn to those who were ultimately destroying him. Can you see Satan's schemes at work here? Physical, mental, emotional, spiritual, relational and financial deterioration, with an ultimate goal of total devastation and destruction.

Consider your own life for a moment. When a thought hits, (remember your ears are a portal to your mind) and you choose to believe that thought, it takes root within your heart. It then manifests through your feelings, words and actions.

The flow-on effect of your feelings, words and actions impacts the people around you in your home, your work, your church and broader community. As well as the direction you take with your finances.

I'm from an accounting background, and so I fully agree with the 'statement' (excuse the pun if you noticed that one) that 'the numbers never lie.' If you want to take a look at the condition of your well-being, look at where your money goes. What are you sowing into? What apps are you subscribed to? What are you watching and listening to? What are you opening yourself up to that is actually creating a new cycle of potential sin and curses? Garbage in, garbage out.

Let's not be the generation that creates generational sin but rather be the generation that breaks it.

PAUSE AND PONDER

Is there anything that's come to mind as you've read these last few pages, that you know you need to bring before the Lord? Jot it down. Do not miss this opportunity to collate everything that needs to be addressed, because together, we are going to do business with our Maker. It's time to draw a line in the sand. The enemy has stolen for long enough. We are a generation of Spirit-led warriors who are not going to sit by and watch the enemy take us out, generation after generation. It's time to take back what is rightfully ours.

CHAPTER 9

LAYING THE FOUNDATION

TEST THE FRUIT

I had to go through the process of breaking curses spoken over me by my narcissistic boss. If you don't know the full story by now, then I really do encourage you to read my previous book, 'The Orange Hue.'

I woke up to Satan's schemes and realised that his method of trying to take me out, was by using the verbal and psychological abuse of my boss to strip me of my identity. Here's the thing. When we lose sight of our identity, we live life in the shadows of our true selves, and not in the fullness of who Papa God has put us on this earth to be. There can only ever be one YOU. If Satan can take YOU out, then that's one less person of potential God-impact that he has to worry about on this earth, and he'll then leave you to implode while he moves on to his next unsuspecting victim. It's time for us to open our eyes to what is going on in the spirit realm, because as Ephesians 6:12 says, 'We wrestle not against flesh and blood…' Have I been completely set free from the curses spoken over me? Absolutely and I even had an opportunity to test it for myself.

My previous boss happened to be at a conference in South Africa that Sandro and I were also attending, and when it dawned on me that I may bump into him, my first reaction was sheer panic. But then I brought it to Papa God, and I prayed in my heart that if I were to see this man again, I would use it as a test to see just how far I had come in my own journey of forgiveness.

Turns out, I didn't bump into him at all throughout the whole conference. Then on closing night, right in the middle of our last session, I received a text message from my sister to say that he had approached her and asked if Sandro and I could meet him in the guest lounge at the end of the session. I could feel my blood drain from my veins as I started to sink lower into my seat, while passing Sandro my handset. I knew deep down that we had to do this.

We were ushered by security into the guest lounge later that evening, and there he was. He seemed smaller than I had remembered, and he was older too. And then as if I left my body, I watched the whole scene unfold from a bird's eye view. Before I could give it a second thought, I found myself running towards him and flinging my arms around him. I gave him an almighty hug and then realised that I had probably never hugged him for as long as I worked for him.

All I felt was immense love, empathy and compassion. That's not something that can happen in the natural after everything that had transpired. It was a supernatural kind of love. My heart was bursting with joy. I had been completely healed and restored of every word spoken over me, every action taken against me, and I felt a blanket of peace come over me. I knew in that moment that all those years of submitting to the process of God healing my heart, I now had healthy fruit to show for it. Now I'm not alluding to everyone running into the arms of their abusers. But what I am saying here is that we have a responsibility to test the fruit that our own lives are producing.

There is always fruit. Be it good or bad, a tree is known by its fruit. The fruit however is determined by the seed sown. This is emphasised in a rather straightforward passage of scripture in Matthew 12:33-37 NKJV which reads:

> *"Either make the tree good and its fruit good, or else make the tree bad and its fruit bad; for a tree is known by its fruit. Brood of vipers! How can you, being evil, speak good things? For out of the abundance of the heart the mouth speaks. A good man out of the good treasure of his heart brings forth good things, and an evil man out of the evil treasure brings forth evil things. But I say to you that for every idle word men may speak, they will give account of it in the day of judgment. For by your words, you will be justified, and by your words you will be condemned."*

What fruit is your life bearing? In order to test the fruit, one must first ask what seeds are being sown by the doors we open. Below are some examples of seeds sown by the doors we open, in and through the six pillars of our lives, that do not originate from the throne room of heaven but rather from the whispers of Satan and the voice and pressures of our fallen world.

1. Spiritual Seeds Sown

Examples include opening doors to the spirit realm while denying Jesus. This is very dangerous because the demonic realm is real. Unfortunately, Satan knows that people are hungry and curious to experience the supernatural, and so he leads the unsuspecting through doors such as free masonry, tarot card and crystal ball reading, séances, occult, new age and witchcraft.

Following any demonic ideology is actually a counterfeit to Jesus. It is deception and only leads to death and separation from Father God. As my precious mama says, 'Be careful not to play in the devils backyard.'

2. Mental Seeds Sown

Examples of seeds sown by the doors we open include anxiety, depression, suicidal thoughts, guilt, shame, condemnation. Believing the lies that you are not good enough, that you don't have what it takes and that you'll never make it. Some of these lies were seeded when you were very young, and by the very people you loved and trusted. Some of these doors were opened unknowingly, yet the lies have taken root within your heart and have formed the basis of your beliefs, feelings, words and actions.

3. Emotional Seeds Sown

Examples include opening doors to imposter syndrome as they call it- where we don't feel worthy of the position we carry. Self-loathing, anger that leads us to doing things we later regret, jealousy, hopelessness, stress, worry, sadness, disappointment, fear, panic, doubt, confusion to name a few.

4. Physical Seeds Sown

Examples of seeds sown by the doors we open include addictions such as gambling, smoking, drugs, alcohol, pornography, masturbation or sex. Other physical actions such as abuse, adultery, murder, rape, domestic violence to name a few. These are physical actions that lead to further destruction. Remember John 10:10 where it says that the thief comes to kill, steal and destroy? We either bear fruit of blessing of cursing, life or death. There is no in-between.

5. Relational Seeds Sown

Examples of seeds sown by the doors we open include entering into toxic or abusive relationships, being unable to maintain healthy relationships, self-sabotage, gender dysphoria, eating disorders, promiscuity, as well as isolating oneself from others.

6. Financial Seeds Sown

Matthew 6:21 NIV says, 'For where your treasure is, there your heart will be also.' Examples of financial seeds sown by the doors we open that ultimately leads to destruction include funding of addictions such as gambling, drugs, alcohol, pornography or prostitution.

POKE THE BEAR

Now that we've taken a closer look at examples of seeds sown in our lives, we're able to make greater sense of the fruit. Sometimes seeds are sown without us even realising it, and it's only when we see the fruit of our lives looking like trails of destruction in our wake, that we wake up to the reality of what we've allowed to take root. I realise that some of what's been addressed above is pretty confronting, and you may be reading this and squirming as you do. That's okay. Papa God is doing a deep work on the inside of your heart. and is exposing some truths because He longs to see you healed, restored and living your life from a place of victory, so that you can have maximum impact for as long as you have breath.

I'm still on my own healing journey. I'm not there yet and probably won't be this side of glory. But I am hungry to be the best version of myself that I can possibly be, for my loved ones and for the people that God has entrusted into my care. I want to pour out what God has poured in.

Part of the healing process is to allow Papa God to "poke the bear". He may be doing this in you right now. Well, He did this very recently in my own life through a man that Sandro and I hold dear, Pastor At Boshoff, a passionate and unapologetic leader, who has established the largest multicultural and multigenerational church in South Africa. He has known our journey and while at a recent event, during worship, I noticed in the corner of my eye him walking towards me. A moment later he poked my left shoulder. I leant in to hear what he had to say, when he asked me out right, 'Are you leading worship in your home church?'

I froze.

Sandro and I had only recently been repositioned within our new church, and so the most accurate of answers was, 'No.' We agreed to talk more after the event, and he returned to his seat. I couldn't concentrate after that. The bear had officially been poked. But why?

What was going on in my heart that I was now so riled? I suddenly felt like my heart was broken and I wanted to burst. Of course, we were in a room of thousands, and it wouldn't have been appropriate for the gushing forth of snot and tears, so I held myself together, but for the duration of the evening I had this internal battle raging. 'Lord, what is going on?' I asked.

During the evening's proceedings, I replayed Pastor At's question, while frantically trying to justify the reasons why I'm not currently leading worship in my home church. Whenever I travel and minister around the world, worship is very much a part of what I do. We had only been in our new church for about a year, and it takes time to find one's footing. But as my thoughts continued to permeate, I realised that the idea of putting myself forward to be a part of the worship team in my new home church left me feeling agitated and uncomfortable. Yikes. Something was afoot, but I just couldn't work out where these unwanted feelings were coming from.

I absolutely love our church and the worship that flows from it. Why on earth wouldn't I want to be a part of that?

Later that evening we were ushered into the guest lounge where Pastor At was seated with other Pastors and dignitaries. When we walked in, he smiled and acknowledged us, and every now and then as the evening progressed and conversations continued, I would see him looking over in our direction. I avoided eye contact at all costs. But then the inevitable happened. 'So, Nalini,' he blurts out while silencing the room as he does. 'When are you going to lead worship in your home church?' Straight up. No fluffing the pillows to make one comfortable. Just out with it.

I sheepishly responded that as we are new to the church, we are still figuring out 'where the Lord wants us,' but to watch this space. He slowly nodded. I knew he knew that the bear had been poked.

DOING BUSINESS WITH GOD

By the time Sandro and I got in the car to head home, the bubbling volcano well and truly erupted. Apparently in volcanic terms, what my heart had been experiencing since the first shoulder poke earlier in the evening is known as a 'gas slug'. Such a glamourous term. The bubbling of lava accumulates and coalesces into large bubbles till it eventually erupts. Interestingly according to Wikipedia, it's the 'agitation' that leads to the 'eruption'. Madam here was certainly agitated and now undergoing a fully-fledged eruption.

Sandro was amazing and knew that I needed time to do business with my Papa God. I found myself leaning on the passenger window just as I had done four years prior when we left the grounds of the rehabilitation centre. Only this time, it was the rugged terrain of Botswana, Africa, set against the backdrop of the very same moon that I frequently gazed at as a little girl when sitting on my dad's shoulders as he walked us home from church.

I asked Papa God to show me what was going on in my heart. I thought I had forgiven my pastor in London, and that the work God needed to do in me was done. I thought this was proven when I came face to face with him, just one year prior to this very moment.

I stared intently at the moon as I waited for Papa God to speak. I then felt Him drop in my spirit, 'It has nothing to do with your pastor in London. All of that has been healed and restored.'

'So, what is it, Lord?' I asked.

Immediately my thoughts returned to a vow I had verbally made to God some years prior. I couldn't believe what I was remembering. It was like God took me straight back to the scene of the crime as it were. There I was, standing in a congregation during worship where I said out loud to God, 'I guess I just have to accept that I will never lead worship in my home church again.'

Wow.

What I didn't realise was that the vow I had made, was seeded from a place of hurt and disappointment. It wasn't from my God. But by me saying it out aloud, I was affirming the seed's right to take root in my heart, and I sealed it in the spirit realm, and it was still there to this day, holding me hostage. I needed to break it to be free of it.

I looked at Sandro and blurted out, 'I know exactly what it is.' After sharing what the Lord had revealed to me, we prayed together, and I repented for what I had said all those years ago, and I asked God to break the hold of those words off my life, so that I could be fully free to do whatever it is that God needed of me. Sandro agreed in prayer with me, and it was done.

People often say to me, 'It can't be that easy.' It's almost like for some, their understanding of how God works is as if He wants to make healing hard for us. Well, He doesn't. He longs for our healing more than we do, and more than we could ever fully realise. He's a good, good Father and wants the best for His kids. It breaks His heart when our lives are short-circuited by the beliefs, words and actions of ourselves and others. He wants us to come home and say, 'Papa, You and I have got some business to tend to.' Oh, and as we open our hearts to what He wants to reveal to us, the process of healing and restoration begins.

And here's the thing. With God, there's nothing that is hidden from Him. But He's such a gentleman, because He will never expose to humiliate. He simply nudges and waits for you to come and sit with Him, and to acknowledge the areas that need addressing. *He* doesn't need to be reminded. He just needs *you* to verbally acknowledge and take responsibility for your own beliefs, words and actions, and then give Him permission to do what only He can do. He forgives and restores. He heals the crevices of our broken hearts, and makes us whole, so that, we can get up and be His hands and feet to our broken world.

STEPPING INTO FREEDOM

Everything shifted for me that night. I felt like a weight had been lifted. A weight I didn't even realise I was carrying. I was completely free to return home to Melbourne, Australia and plug in to my new home church in a way that I had not yet done.

Papa God knows that we live in a world that likes to sow seeds of doubt in our minds, and while this is why we need to take our thoughts captive, sometimes He brings confirmation when we need to be reminded of the work that He has done.

We had hardly arrived back in the country when we were attending an event in our new home church. At the end of the event people were given an opportunity to write down anything that needed to be addressed or confessed before God, and then they were encouraged to step out of their seats and bring their pieces of paper to a near life-sized cross that stood at the foot of the stage.

I knew in my heart that I needed to bring what Papa God had revealed to me just a few nights prior, in the moonlight as I gazed over the African terrain. And so, I scribbled down the words, 'I renounce the vow I made that I would never lead worship in my home church again,' I got up and made my way to the cross. There, on my own, I thanked God for hearing my prayer back in Africa, and for confirming to me in that moment that I was completely free. I ripped up the piece of paper and watched it fall around the cross.

Pastors were ready and waiting to pray for each person who stepped forward. The pastor who prayed for me has become a dear friend of mine, but she'd had no idea of what had just happened in Botswana a few nights prior. As we prayed together, with her eyes closed she said, 'There's something that you need to let go of. A vow you made? Something you promised that you would never do?' I laughed as I told her it was done and dealt with at the cross.

Papa God used that encounter to re-confirm to me that the work He needed to do in my heart was complete. He had broken my self-inflicted curse, and I was no longer hostage to my own words. Thank You Jesus.

You may be reading this and scenes in your own life may be bubbling to the surface. Beliefs that have taken root in your heart that you have maybe declared over yourself. Certain conversations you've had, and maybe even words that you've spoken over other people in your world.

Self-cursing holds as much power as cursing towards and from others. But the power of Jesus's blood is *stronger*. That's why He died upon the cross. To break the curse of sin and death.

In the book, 'Intercessory Prayer' by Dutch Sheets, he perfectly articulates the message I need you to understand here. Take your time to digest this because it is life altering.

This is what he says: -

"An interesting word is used in 1 John 3:8 KJV, that adds insight to what happened at the Cross. The verse reads, 'For this purpose the Son of God was manifested, that He might destroy the works of the devil.'

Destroy is the Greek word, *luo*, which has both a legal and a physical meaning. Understanding its full definition will greatly enhance our knowledge of what Jesus did to Satan and his works.

The legal meaning of *luo* is (1) to pronounce or determine that something or someone is no longer bound; (2) to dissolve or void a contract or anything that legally binds. Jesus came to dissolve the legal hold Satan had over us, and to pronounce that we were no longer bound by his works. He 'voided the contract,' breaking his dominion over us.

The physical meaning of *luo* is to dissolve or melt, break, beat something to pieces, or untie something that is bound. In Acts 27:41 the boat Paul travelled on was broken to pieces *(luo)* by the force of a storm. In 2 Peter 3:10,12 we're told that one day the elements of the earth will melt or dissolve *(luo)* from a great heat. Jesus not only delivered us legally, but He also made certain the literal consequences of that deliverance were manifested: He brought healing, set captives free, lifted oppression and liberated those under demonic control."

Dutch Sheets then goes on to point out that Jesus uses the same word, *luo*, to describe what we, the Church, are to do through spiritual warfare as depicted in Matthew 16:19 which reads, 'I will give you the keys of the kingdom of heaven; and whatever you shall bind on earth shall be bound in heaven, and whatever you shall loose on earth shall be loosed in heaven.' The word loose is *luo*.

And if your mind hasn't been completely blown already, Dutch Sheets goes on to say, "Although Jesus fully accomplished the task of breaking the authority of Satan and voiding his legal hold upon the human race, someone on earth must represent Him in that victory and enforce it."

In other words, we don't have to live under generational sin and curses. We hold the authority through Jesus, to represent what He already did at Calvary, by stepping out in victory and completely disarming the continued chit chatter and lies of Satan, and turn not only our lives around, but completely re-write the trajectory of our future generations.

The overflow of stepping into my freedom has only just begun, and its ripple effect is already taking my breath away. I've written my first full-length album in ten years. An album that I've been able to weave within the pages of this book, that I have been penning at a pace I never thought was possible. My 'Unlock Your True Identity' Transformational Program is setting women free around the world. I never thought I would ever create something like that, let alone witness God releasing His healing power through it as a result.

I'm traveling the world sharing stories and songs of the unquenchable love of Jesus, just as I desired at the tender age of four. The 'Under the Rug' Podcast is making waves and is mobilizing Christians to be active agents of change, embodying the hands and feet of Jesus to drive societal reform. Who would have thought that God could use a kid born on a table in Chandigarh, India, who would submit to the painstaking process of His refiner's fire, and come out the other side, still usable?

If God can lead me to freedom, He can certainly do the same for you. But know this, your freedom is not just for you. It's for the ripple effect that *will* take place whether you asked for it or not. So, brace yourself. The radical, transformative shift in you will be too obvious for anyone to ignore. And as with my own experience, some will either be repelled by the change in you, or they will be drawn to it. Either way, grab everything that God has for you with both hands, because you were born for such a time as this, and He needs you as His agent on this earth in this very day.

PAUSE AND PONDER

What has this chapter stirred within your heart? Write it down. Add it to the screeds of notes you've probably already taken since you started this book.

Now, take a deep breath in, because through the appropriation of the blood of Jesus, you are about to be equipped with the tools to overcome generational bondage and rewrite your family's future.

CHAPTER 10

FORTIFYING THE PILLARS

SALVATION – THE BLOODLINE BREAKER

So, how do you strengthen and fortify the six pillars in your life in order to identify and break generational sins and curses in your bloodline, so that your future generations are blessed as well as functioning at optimum levels, and able to live in the fullness of who God created you to be?

I believe you are already getting a sense of the how-tos, but this is exactly what we are going to unpack in greater depth in this final chapter of activation.

I have come across too many people who believe that because their grandmother and mother died of cancer, that they too will die of cancer. I've heard alcoholics say that there is no hope for them because their dad was an alcoholic, and they too have the alcoholic's gene. I've sat with people who believe that because mental health issues run in their family, that there's no escape for their own battles with depression, anxiety and suicidal tendencies.

No, no, no. That is NOT truth! It's time to break free from suffocating beliefs and come into the realisation of the authority you carry as a child of the King. And if you're not yet a child of the King and have not yet accepted Jesus as your Lord and Saviour, then this is the very first step, and we can take it together right now.

You see, salvation is about recognizing that the blood of Jesus has the power to break every generational chain. When we say yes to Jesus, we're not just securing a place in heaven, we're inviting His blood to cleanse our bloodline, to break the patterns of sin that have run through our family for generations, and to make us whole. Salvation is the moment we acknowledge *Jesus, I need You. I believe Your blood is stronger than anything in my past, and I choose You to rewrite my future.*

This is where everything shifts. This is where the curse ends, and redemption begins.

The Bible is clear in Romans 10:9 NIV, 'If you declare with your mouth, 'Jesus is Lord,' and believe in your heart that God raised Him from the dead, you *will* be saved.' If, as you read these words, your heart is stirring, then all you have to do is simply pray this prayer out aloud, and believe in your heart that Father God in Heaven hears you:

Dear Heavenly Father,

I come to you in the Name of Jesus. I believe that Jesus is Your Son and He died on the cross to take away my sins. So, I ask You to forgive me of all of my sins.

I believe that Jesus rose from the grave to give me eternal life. Today I step into right relationship with you through my faith in Jesus, and His completed work on the cross.

I am now Your child.

So, I ask You Lord Jesus to come into my heart, come into my life, become my Lord, my Saviour and my Best Friend.

In Jesus Name I pray,
Amen.

If you prayed this prayer, my team and I would love to hear from you. Our contact details are at the end of this book. But for now, I want to say congratulations on the best decision you could ever make in your life.

You are now about to embark on a journey of utter transformation. In fact, write today's date on the top of this very page. You will look back in years to come, and you'll be able to say, 'This was the moment when everything changed.'

At the start of this book, I promised to take you on a very personal journey while unwrapping intimate details from my own life, so that you could begin to see the stitching of a magnificent love-story come into formation. It is my hope that as the story has unfolded, you have been able to connect certain parts of your own story and interweave it with mine.

I had no idea that my son's diagnosis, and the link to my brother's death, would lead me on a journey of standing in the gap through the power of Jesus, to break generational sins and curses off my family's bloodline, in order to release and spare future generations from those same sins and curses.

Salvation is the first step to fortifying the Six Pillars of The Human Life that I describe in this book. We are spiritual beings having a human experience, and so the condition of your spirit-being is critical to your wellbeing as a whole. Why? Because you and I were made first and foremost, to have fellowship with Papa God. Without Him, life is empty. You go through the motions of eat, sleep, work, family, friends, hobbies, repeat. But for what? What's the deeper meaning of it all? Where's the deeper purpose? Your deeper purpose is found in God, and God alone.

When your spirit-being is bonded to God, as you grow in your understanding of His nature and character, more is revealed as to your own identity, and to what God has purposed for you to do and complete on this earth before your time comes to cross into eternity, to be with Him forevermore. And I'll tell you now, your life on this earth is way more than eat, sleep, work, family, friends, hobbies, repeat. But it's like a treasure hunt. You have to seek it out to find it.

SURRENDER – THE NEXT STEP

Salvation is the starting point, but surrender is the journey. It's one thing to receive Jesus as Lord, it's another to follow Him. So, what is the next step in surrender? **Baptism.**

Baptism is more than just a symbolic act – it's a declaration to the spirit realm. It's saying, *I'm dying to my old self, my old ways, my old bloodline, and I am rising into the new life Jesus has for me.* It's a physical step that represents a spiritual shift. An outward expression, of an inward transformation. It's also an act of obedience, a public declaration of faith, and a spiritual marker of our new identity in Christ. Jesus Himself commanded baptism as part of the Great Commission which we read in Matthew 28:19-20 NKJV, 'Go therefore and make disciples of all the nations, baptizing them in the name of the Father and of the Son and of the Holy Spirit, teaching them to observe all things that I have commanded you; and lo, I am with you always, even to the end of the age.'

Once we receive His salvation and step out in obedience through baptism, we are positioning ourselves before God, our Maker, and saying, 'Lord, I'm all in.' Then we can boldly come before Him to seek out our purpose and find it. You haven't been put on this earth just to survive. You are here for such a time as this, and God wants to use your life for His glory.

How do we discover our God-given purpose? Through time spent in His presence. But like in the process of forming any new habit, a journey is required. One that starts off as structured discipline and gradually transforms into a deep-rooted dedication. When someone sets out to become fit and healthy, it isn't simply a matter of wishing for change; it demands intentional action. The body must transition from shoving in processed junk food, to being nourished by whole, life-giving foods. What begins as a strict regimen of dragging oneself to the gym – pushing through soreness, fatigue, and discomfort – eventually gives way to an internal shift. Over time, the body itself starts to crave the movement, the challenge, the vitality that exercise brings. What once felt like an obligation now becomes a source of inspiration and joy.

This same principle applies in our relationship with God. The pursuit of intimacy with Him doesn't happen by accident; it requires investment on your part. God Himself says in Jeremiah 29:13 NKJV, 'And you will seek Me and find Me, when you search for Me with all your heart.' The seeking must be intentional, persistent, and wholehearted. At first, carving out time for prayer and reading the Bible may feel structured, even forced. Waking up early to sit in His presence may very well be a battle against the flesh. But as we remain consistent, something shifts within. This isn't about creating rules and regulations for one to squeeze into. It's about nurturing your relationship with God to the point where you're able to identify His voice in the thick of opposition.

Over time, the spirit awakens before the body, stirring us from sleep with a yearning to be with our King. What once required discipline becomes a delight. The hunger for His presence becomes stronger than the resistance of our physical bodies. We no longer engage out of duty, but out of desire. Just as a healthy body thrives on movement and nourishment, our spirit flourishes in communion with our Lord.

This transformation – from regimented effort to joyful pursuit – is the hallmark of every meaningful change. Whether in fitness or faith, the journey begins with discipline and transforms into devotion.

For Sandro and me, we spend time with the Lord individually, first thing every single morning. I have my cosy couch, and Sandro has his. We both have our own books piled high. I have my Bible, and he has his. I have my journal, and he has his. I also have a book on the go, and miraculously, my non-reading husband is now turning into an avid reader himself! I have my favourite Bic four-colour pen, and Sandro has his.

I start off by envisioning in my mind's eye; Holy Spirit sitting beside me with Jesus, and Papa God sitting opposite me. It's basically me in the wardrobe all over again. God has literally been waiting for our cuppa and chinwag together. (British slang for tea and talk). I use what's described as the ACTS model in my times with Him. It's helped provide structure and now flows so easily I don't even think about it.

1. Adoration

The first few words that come out of my mouth are words of adoration before Him. Not because God has an identity crisis, but because the more I magnify Him, and focus my attention on who He is and how great He is, the circumstances around me shrink back down to size. He is put in His rightful place, as the highest authority within my life, and everything else dims in comparison.

Take a moment right now to adore your King of Kings. Picture Him on His throne, and you as His precious child, coming before Him, in awe of who He is to you personally. Declare out aloud in your own words, your adoration. For example: Oh God, I love You. You are worthy to be praised. You are King above all kings. You are Lord above all lords. There is none like You. You hold the highest position of authority in my life. Your heart longs for the hearts of humanity. Your heart breaks at man's resistance towards you. But God, I adore You. I lay my life down before You, and I take this moment to worship You.'

Then I pause, I wait, and I listen. God always responds to a heart that leans in. Sometimes I hear the birds singing their own worship before God. Other times, it's the leaves of the trees clapping their hands before Him. I pause, I wait, and I listen. Holy Spirit drops a picture in my mind's eye, and I grab my journal to capture it. Or sometimes it's a scripture, or the name of a loved one who I know I need to check in with. Every time I pause, wait and listen, God responds.

2. Confession

After my time of adoration, I take a moment in confession. The Lord says in 1 John 1:9 NKJV, 'If we confess our sins, He is faithful and just and will forgive us our sins and purify us from all unrighteousness.' I don't want anything to stand in the way of my relationship with God. You know that yuck feeling, when you've had a fight with a loved one. There's tension in the air that you know needs sorting. I don't want that tension or awkwardness with Papa God. So, I keep short accounts with Him. If there is anything that I've done or said that is displeasing to Him, I bring it before Him and I apologise. I ask for His forgiveness, knowing that He is a God of His word, and forgives and purifies me from the inside out. Then I can move on.

It doesn't mean that because God forgives, that He's giving us free license to do what we want. No. That's a totally warped perspective of His love, mercy and grace. Saying sorry means that you admit to having done wrong, and that you choose to turn around. In some cases, the turnaround requires God's supernatural intervention, because we cannot do it our own strength. That's okay, all you have to do is ask Him for His intervention. And He will give it freely.

Why not take a moment right now. Pause, reflect, and if anything comes to mind, lay it at the foot of the cross, say sorry and ask the Lord for forgiveness. Then pause, wait and listen. I quite often feel a sense of peace in this moment.

3. Thanksgiving

Then I take time to give thanks. I'm so thankful to Him for everything He's done in my life. For how He's never given up on me. For loving me and believing in me, even when I didn't love or believe in myself. I thank Him for my precious husband, and my sons. For loving them, protecting them, nurturing and guiding them. For seeing us all through some very dark days. What are you thankful to Him for? What has He done in your life that you just have to take a moment, right now, to give Him thanks?

Then, pause, wait and listen. I quite often find myself smiling in this moment. It's as if everything stops. There's a stillness in the air, and I feel the warmth of His magnificent presence.

4. Supplication

After my time of adoration, confession and thanksgiving, I find my heart is in a posture of humility before my King. I'm humbled that He, the Creator of the Universe, cares so much to spend time with me. It's in this posture that I can now come before Him in supplication. This is when I bring my requests before Him.

Philippians 4:6-8 NKJV says, 'Be anxious for nothing, but in everything by prayer and supplication, with thanksgiving, let your requests be made known to God, and the peace of God, which surpasses all understanding, will guard your hearts and minds through Christ Jesus.'

Papa God wants the issues you face to be brought to Him. He longs for your surrender, where you admit that you cannot do it alone. He's a good, good Father, and He wants to be your rescuer. What are you facing right now, that you're struggling to carry the weight of? Why not take a moment right now to close your eyes and give it all to Jesus. Lay it at the foot of the cross and ask for supernatural intervention. Then breathe. You're a child of the King, and He loves you. Even when you don't have the answers, He does.

Once I've had my prayer time, I eat from His Word. I ask Holy Spirit to give me wisdom to understand the mysteries written within its pages.

So, here's my challenge to you. Where is your cosy space to spend time with your Lord and King? Where do you sit with Him, talk with Him, commune with Him? What does it look like for you? Is it a specific spot in your home, or is it a walk and talk along the beach? Are you a garden stroller, or a mountain climber? Wherever it is for you, commit to making that place your very own wardrobe.

And then, *decide* on a time and stick to it. As I mentioned before, for Sandro and me, we want to give Him the first fruits of our day, so before I even make the bed in the morning, I'm in my cosy dressing gown and fluffy bedroom slippers, with my spirit bouncing on the inside of me, with eager anticipation to meet with my God. And just like forming any new habit, it first requires discipline. Just as your body doesn't become ripped with muscles by *thinking* about joining the gym. You have to commit to showing up to the gym and doing the hard work. It's no different with time spent with our God.

Once you have found your spot, close your eyes and catch your breath for a moment. Inhale His most beautiful presence and then use the ACTS model that you have learned.

Each day in His presence is different. Linger. Don't rush your time with Him. Every moment is precious.

The beauty of a close relationship with God is you don't have to carry the burdens of life and circumstances on your own shoulders. You're able to hand them over to Jesus and He carries them for you. The fortifying of the six pillars in our lives stems from the fortifying of our spirit-being. When our spirit-being is strong and grounded in God, all hell can break loose around you, but you will be able to stand firm, because you know who you are, whose you are and, who fights for you.

SUBMISSION

Papa God does not reveal things when we are not yet ready to face them. That's why walking with Him is like being on a treasure hunt. The more you seek after Him, the more you find. Allow me to ratify Jeremiah 29:13 NKJV, 'And you will seek Me and find Me, when you search for Me with all your heart.'

I had to purposefully and intentionally seek God out when my son was diagnosed with the same illness that killed my brother. I had to hear directly from heaven as to what we were to do.

Here's the crazy thing! According to the doctors, this particular illness manifests in boys between the ages of five and seven. Children with this illness do not usually live past seven years of age. Björn was only *diagnosed* when he turned *thirteen*. Had he been diagnosed at age five, it would have been right in the middle of the traumatic season that we as a family were facing in London. You can learn more about this story in my first book, 'The Orange Hue.' I absolutely believe, without a shadow of a doubt, that the Lord allowed my son's illness to remain dormant until the right time. Was I ready for any of it when it hit? No, of course not. But God knew that we were, and He knew that as long as we drew strength from Him, we would position ourselves on the frontlines of battle and be able to stand firm.

It was God who revealed to me the connection between hereditary illnesses and generational curses in the Bible. It then set in motion the mama-bear within me, to seek God out for answers on behalf of my child. I didn't realise that the snowball effect would be a book called 'Bloodline,' and that what God has revealed in and through our own journey, is now setting people free from generational sins and curses, all around the world.

You see, there is always a bigger picture at play when Papa God is in the equation. I think back to 'The Orange Hue', and while what we endured was brutal, if we hadn't gone through all of that and learnt tenacity, endurance, resilience and reliance on God in the heat of battle, as well as forgiveness on the other side of battle, I don't think we would have coped facing our boy's health crisis, let alone his drug addiction, and my mental health crash.

Sometimes however, it's when we journey through the valley seasons that our hearts become hard like stone. This is when Papa God has to do open heart surgery on us first, before we are ready and 'open' for what else He wants and needs to reveal to us, in order for us to be completely healed and set free.

Once your heart is soft and ready to receive what's next, Papa God does so gently, in your language, and at a pace that He knows you can handle. This is how I've seen Him do it in my own life. He gradually begins by highlighting areas within the six pillars that require attention. And even though what He reveals can at times be confronting, as long as we surrender and submit to the process, His revelation, coupled with our surrender, brings forth His healing.

This is when Psalm 119:105 NKJV brings so much comfort to my soul. 'Your word is a lamp to my feet and a light to my path.'

Papa God doesn't shine a spotlight on you, blinding you in the process. Instead, He shines a quirky little lamp, with just enough light to show you the next step immediately in front of you.

He may reveal doors that you have opened in the spirit-realm, that need to be closed. Even those doors that were opened in childlike curiosity years ago, that Satan has used as a foothold in your life, without you even realising it, can be shut.

'I know that you wouldn't have done it with malicious intent. In fact, you wouldn't have known what you were doing at the time'

That's okay. It's still an open door, nonetheless. It must, and can be closed, under the authority of Jesus. An authority that *you* now carry.

Papa God may reveal to you areas in your mind, will and emotions that need to fall under His authority, His healing power and His Holy Spirit anointing. Again, with a softness of heart, as you surrender to His gentle nudging and leading, you are saying, 'Lord, I give You permission to do Your work in me, from the inside out.' Papa God is the perfect gentleman. He will never force your hand. He waits patiently for you to grant Him access to your heart.

There may be physical behaviours that Papa God will challenge you about. It could be one morning during your cosy time with Him, that He drops into your spirit, 'My child, this behaviour cannot go on any longer.' Or certain addictions that you've struggled to break in your own strength.

May I remind you of Zechariah 4:6 NKJV which reads, '…Not by might nor by power, *but by My Spirit* says the Lord of hosts.'

Some addictions cannot be broken just by sheer willpower. Some require supernatural intervention from God on high. Why battle with it alone, when you can submit it under the authority of Jesus and have HIM fight *for* you? Yes, it's still a partnership. You still have to take responsibility, and put boundaries in place and remain accountable, but you do not have to face it alone without supernatural support and strength from your God. There is a call to purity that is taking place across the earth, and within the body of Christ. Papa God is coming back for His *pure* Bride. One without spot or blemish. But He doesn't expect perfection from us. He longs for us to come to Him in our wounded state, so that He alone can heal, restore and perfect us, and then He alone gets all the glory.

There may be times when Papa God highlights certain relationships in your life that are not healthy for your future. This can be a very painful revelation, but remember, God doesn't reveal anything to harm you. He only wants what's best for you. He is a good, good Father, and He loves you.

You may be facing financial struggles right now. When you surrender your finances to God, He highlights areas where there is a lack of stewardship. He may challenge you with how you spend your money. There is a term, 'the numbers never lie.' Having an accounting background myself, I know this to be true. You only have to look at one's bank account to know where one's heart lies. When we can be trusted with a little, He is faithful to entrust us with more. Maybe it's time to surrender and submit your bank account to Him, so He can bring revelation from the throne room of Heaven. And when you choose to partner with Him by stepping out in obedience to His promptings, watch and see the floodgates open.

Has there ever been a time when you've found yourself saying to a loved one something like, 'If you thought that of me, then you really don't know me at all.' Its' like this with Papa God. Sometimes we form a narrative in our minds of who He is and what He's like, and we make Him out to be the enemy.

He's not the old, angry, judgemental God who's waving his rod around, ready to beat the living daylights out of anyone who steps out of line. He's not to be compared to earthly fathers who abuse their positions of authority. No. That's not what Papa God is like at all. And if you think that of Him, then you really don't know Him. In which case, I urge you to re-read this book all over again. Look for the threads of His loving kindness woven within my story. Allow Him to reveal to you moments in your own life where He stepped in on your behalf. Because when you are set free from humanising God, suddenly His magnitude is awakened within your spirit, and every pillar of your life stands the chance of being radically transformed. Your spiritual, mental, emotional, physical, relational and financial pillars matter to God, and are strengthened and fortified in Him.

SPIRITUAL WARFARE

God's objective for your life has always been to transform you into the person that He had originally mapped out for you, when He first designed you. I've always imagined the most ornate boardroom in heaven where I see Papa God, Jesus and Holy Spirit standing with intent excitement around a solid oak table. Papa God rolls out a scroll of gold graph paper that contains the architectural plans of your life. There at the top of the scroll is your name, etched in the finest of calligraphy. The plans contain intricate detail of every facet of your being. Your looks, your personality, your quirks and heart's desires. Oh, and how magnificent you are. Papa God, Jesus and Holy Spirit, as a triune Godhead, smile in anticipation for the day of your birth, and for the life you will live, and the lives you will change.

You are then born into a fallen world, and from the day of your birth, Satan and his cohorts have had their own objective for your life.

To take you out.

To kill, steal and destroy any possible encounter, let alone intimate relationship, between you and Papa God. They know all too well that when you know your Heavenly Father, you will know yourself. And when you know yourself and what God has purposed for your life, you will become a force to be reckoned with on this earth and will do catastrophic damage to the kingdom of darkness.

Your encounter with Jesus takes place, and you begin to hunger for more of God, like never before. In fact, you're not naturally an early riser, but you find yourself waking up earlier and earlier, not because your physical body is ready to wake up, but because your spirit-being is stirring for time with its Maker.

Then Papa God prompts, nudges and pokes. You feel convicted within your spirit. Conviction is good, and is from God, because it leads to Godly sorrow, which in turn leads to repentance and ultimately reform. This is highlighted in 2 Corinthians 7:10 NIV 'Godly sorry brings repentance that leads to salvation and leaves no regret, but worldly sorrow brings death.' Romans 12:2 NKJV says 'And do not be conformed to this world, but be transformed by the renewing of your mind, that you may prove what is that good and acceptable and perfect will of God.'

While Satan failed in his attempts to stop your blossoming relationship with God, he still comes at you with condemnation. The Spirit of God convicts while Satan condemns. Conviction leads to change, whilst condemnation leads to guilt and shame.

Romans 8:1 NIV says, 'Therefore, there is now *no condemnation* for those who are in Christ Jesus.' So, even during your quiet times with Papa God, as He reveals truth to you, be aware that the enemy prowls around as depicted in 1 Peter 5:8 NIV which reads, 'Be alert and of sober mind. Your enemy the devil prowls around like a roaring lion looking for someone to devour.'

The enemy likes to pounce when you least expect it, and he'll go for any one of the six pillars in your life. He will target you physically, mentally, emotionally, spiritually, relationally and financially. We don't have to fear his schemes, because we know that our God is greater than anything the enemy can throw at us. But we do have to be vigilant and awake, ready and prepared for spiritual warfare when called for. Part of that vigilance is to discern the voice of God, versus the sly, deceptive voice of the enemy. When you feel challenged on a matter, ask yourself, 'Is this conviction, or is this condemnation that I am picking up right now?'

Godly conviction awakens a supernatural fire within your belly that quickens you to rise up and initiate change. However, when condemnation comes knocking, what you experience is a surge of fear, guilt or shame that begins to torment you, and bubbles up on the inside. This is when you need to take a proactive step in spiritual warfare, in order to rebuke and silence the enemy's attempts at sabotage.

The enemy likes us to lick our wounds, and to make us feel less-than. Say for instance Papa God is challenging you on a specific addiction that has held you captive for some time. The enemy will want to warp your receptors, and wrap your thoughts in guilt and shame, where you're too embarrassed to address the matter before God. He used that very same tactic with Adam and Eve in the garden of Eden, because he wants you to hide in shame.

Genesis 3:8 NKJV reads, 'And they heard the sound of the Lord God walking in the garden in the cool of the day, and Adam and his wife hid themselves from the presence of the Lord God among the trees of the garden.'

For as long as you are hiding in shame, the matter remains buried under the rug, and you become of no effect to the Kingdom of God, nor to the breaking of sin and curses in your life, let alone your family's lives, and the lives of your future generations. Can you see the catastrophic ripple effect of succumbing to the enemy's sabotaging schemes?

What do you do when the enemy comes at you? What does spiritual warfare actually look like?

Spiritual warfare is not passive. It is active. It requires you to get up, dress up, stand to attention, and fight as God instructs, while leaving the victory of that fight in the Hands of God.

Picture an actual battlefield of old, like that of World War II. But instead of physically going out to war, you are armoured up in the Spirit. The minute you surrender your life to Jesus; you enter a spiritual battle. Remember, the enemy hates your connection with God. You're of no threat to Satan when you don't know God. But the minute you surrender to God in Heaven, you become a target. So how do you prepare for spiritual warfare? Well, you have to get dressed for war!

The passage in the Bible that talks about the armour of God is found in Ephesians 6:10-18 and here it is from *The Voice* translation:

Finally, *brothers and sisters,* draw your strength and might from God. Put on the full armour of God to protect yourselves from the devil and his evil schemes. We're not waging war against enemies of flesh and blood alone. No, this fight is against tyrants, against authorities, against *supernatural* powers *and demon princes that slither* in the darkness of this world, and against wicked *spiritual armies* that lurk about in heavenly places.

And this is why you need *to be head-to-toe in* the full armour of God: so, you can resist during these evil days and be fully prepared to hold your ground. Yes, stand—truth banded around your waist, righteousness as your chest plate, and feet protected in preparation to proclaim the good news of peace. Don't forget to raise the shield of faith above all else, so you will be able to extinguish flaming spears hurled at you from the wicked one. Take also the helmet of salvation and the sword of the Spirit, which is the word of God. Pray always. Pray in the Spirit. Pray about everything in every way you know how! And keeping all this in mind, pray on behalf of God's people. Keep on praying feverishly and be on the lookout *until evil has been stayed.*'

One of the best books I've ever read on being armoured up and ready for spiritual warfare is called 'Armed and Dangerous' by Evangelist Tim Hall. If you haven't read it, maybe this needs to be your next read during your wardrobe moments with Jesus.

Once you are armoured up in the spirit, strategic prayer and worship are critical components to spiritual warfare. There are certain mountains we face that cannot be moved without fervent prayer and worship.

Time spent in prayer and worship gives passage for me to come before my Father in adoration, thanksgiving, repentance and to then submit my requests before Him and to wait on Him for His response. What I have come to experience for myself, is a sharpening of my spiritual senses. The same way we have physical senses – sight, hearing, taste, smell, and touch, so we have spiritual senses.

1. Spiritual Sight

Eyes to see and discern what is taking place in both the physical and spiritual realm. Psalm 119:18 NKJV reads, 'Open my eyes, that I may see wondrous things from Your law.' Suddenly passages of scripture jump out of the pages of the Bible as Holy Spirit brings revelation, and suddenly our spirit understands what has been written. I can walk into a room and the hair on the back of my neck stands to attention because I can see demonic influences at play, and so I'm ready, on guard, and vigilant to what's going on around me. But I can only see this because of time spent with my Lord and King, where He sharpens my spiritual sight and discernment.

2. Spiritual Hearing

Hearing allows us to process sound and communication. John 10:27 NKJV, 'My sheep hear My voice, and I know them, and they follow Me.' Our times with the Lord must include moments of silence where we listen for His still, soft voice. I do this by closing my eyes and just waiting on Him. Sometimes a song will drop into my spirit, and I'll quietly begin to sing. Other times a picture comes to mind, or a person's name. When I am seeking the Lord for strategy, as I wait on Him, He gives me the blueprint, the next step. Boom. Out of nowhere I know exactly what I need to do. If you're in a situation right now where you need Godly wisdom, drop everything, and go and spend time with your Lord in your wardrobe. Sit and listen.

3. Spiritual Taste

Taste allows us to savour and enjoy flavours. Psalm 34:8 NKJV, 'Oh, taste and see that the Lord is good; Blessed is the man who trusts in Him!' We have so much to be thankful for. Our God is such a good, good, Father. I believe there are miracles that have taken place in your life that you are not even aware of. But what of the ones you are? How has God come through for you in the past? As you take a moment to meditate on all that He has done for you, can you not taste His sweet goodness? Children of the King should be the happiest, friendliest people on the planet. We have so much to be grateful for, we have no right to complain. If the fruit of what flows out of your mouth, your body-language, and the way you treat your loved ones is full of entitlement, negativity, despair, despondency, disillusionment, then you need to get yourself into the wardrobe, close the door, and come before your heavenly Father. Adore Him, confess attitudes and behaviours before Him, spend time giving thanks to Him for everything He has done. Do not leave that wardrobe until all negativity dissipates. Then, step out of the wardrobe clothed in a garment of praise.

Isaiah 61:1-3 NKJV, 'The Spirit of the Lord GOD *is* upon Me, Because the LORD has anointed Me to preach good tidings to the poor; He has sent Me to heal the broken-hearted, to proclaim liberty to the captives, and the opening of the prison to *those who are* bound; To proclaim the acceptable year of the LORD, And the day of vengeance of our God; To comfort all who mourn, To console those who mourn in Zion, To give them beauty for ashes, The oil of joy for mourning, The garment of praise for the spirit of heaviness; That they may be called trees of righteousness, The planting of the LORD, that He may be glorified.'

4. Spiritual Smell

Smell connects us to memories and emotions through scents. I'm reminded of 2 Corinthians 2:15 NKJV, 'For we are to God the fragrance of Christ among those who are being saved and among those who are perishing.' When we walk into a room, the scent we give off must be that which is warm and inviting. If you walk into a room, and the scent you give off is that of a smelly sock, who are you representing? Because that isn't our Jesus! He *drew* crowds to Himself. Even the ones who hated Him were constantly hovering around Him. People should be curious about you. How is it that you are filled with so much joy, when you have been through so much sorrow? Ah, well it's the joy of the Lord that's your strength. May His joy exude from every facet of your being.

5. Spiritual Touch

Touch allows us to feel and connect physically. Jesus often touched those He healed. There is power in physical connection. Matthew 8:3 NKJV, 'Then Jesus put out His hand and touched him, saying, "I am willing; be cleansed." Immediately his leprosy was cleansed.'

When we extend our hands to someone, we are releasing God's comfort, healing and tangible presence. This is why we lay hands on people when we pray for them. Out of you flows rivers of His living water, and by your touch, you are transferring that flow.

Oh, may we as children of the King, begin to understand the power of God that we have access to in our day to day lives, and became more intentional about putting that power into practice. As we do, our world will begin to look very different.

If you are reading this, then I believe that deep down within your heart, you have a desire to be used powerfully by God. Well, I'm here to tell you that you can be, and He *wants* you to be. You hold, and have access to, His supernatural power that is released when we seek our God, surrender to Him, and submit to whatever He needs to do within us, to mould and shape us for His glory. He will not entrust His supernatural power into the hands of those who will abuse it. That would be catastrophic. It would be like allowing an eighteen-year-old to drive a Mercedes GT Sports. It would be a death sentence, giving that amount of power to an immature adult. And if you know the power within you but have not yet been released to function at your fullness, be encouraged. This day will come. Do not despise the days of small beginnings. Look at the size of an oak tree, in comparison to the size of its seed when it first germinated. Galatians 6:9 AMP, 'Let us not grow weary *or* become discouraged in doing good, for at the proper time we will reap, if we do not give in.'

It's time to step into the fullness of who you are as a child of the King. A warrior with courage and might. One who stands on the battlefield, armoured up, and ready to take back the ground that the enemy has stolen.

STANDING IN THE GAP

In Chapter 9, I gave some examples of seeds that were sown by some of the doors we can open in The Six Pillars of a Human Life, that do not originate from the throne room of heaven, but rather from the whispers of Satan and the voice and pressures of this fallen world.

This book, Bloodline, has been setting you up for this very moment. You are about to be activated as a warrior in the spirit, in order to bridge or stand in the gap for yourself, your loved ones and your future generations. I encourage you to be in your wardrobe moment with the Lord, as you undertake the steps provided below. Couples, I encourage you to do this together, so that you can stand in agreement with one another. If you're single, but you have a friend whom you can call on to bear witness on your behalf, then do that. There is weight when two or more agree. However, if you're on your own, ask Holy Spirit to bear witness with you.

This is not something that you step into light-heartedly or frivolously. This is about positioning and petitioning the King of all kings and must be done with humility and thankfulness of heart.

You are about to be equipped with weapons to break generational sins and curses off your own life, as well as bridge the gap on behalf of your future generations, through the power of Jesus. Are you ready?

Buckle up.

Have your Bible, journal and pen to hand. Start by spending some time in worship. Put on one of your favourite worship songs, and sing along. Ready your heart. Welcome Holy Spirit and ask Him to bring fresh revelation as you sit with Him. Ask Him to show you specific areas in your life that need to be addressed. Take a moment to adore, confess, and give thanks to the Lord.

When you are ready, you are going to work through each of the six pillars from the standpoint of your salvation in God, your surrender and submission to His change-process, while being armoured up and positioned for spiritual warfare.

It's as though you are standing before God as a lawyer, advocating on behalf of you and your loved ones. Picture yourself standing in the Court Room of Heaven. Holy Spirit is your guide and helper, Jesus is interceding on your behalf, and Papa God, your King, is Judge.

1. Spiritual Pillar

As mentioned in Chapter 9, examples of seeds sown in our spiritual lives include opening doors to the spirit realm, while denying Jesus. This is very dangerous, because the demonic realm is real. Unfortunately, Satan knows that people are hungry and curious to experience supernatural power, and so he leads unsuspecting victims through doors such as free masonry, tarot card and crystal ball reading, séances, occult, new age and witchcraft. Following any demonic ideology is actually a counterfeit to Jesus. It is deception and only leads to death and separation from Papa God. As my precious mama always says, 'Be careful not to play in the devil's backyard.'

If Holy Spirit is highlighting any doors that may have been opened unintentionally in the spirit realm, be it you personally, or generations before you, you have the authority to come before God to confess and close those doors that may have been opened within your bloodline.

As you step into His Royal Court, dressed and ready for spiritual warfare, through the power of prayer, you are about to bridge the gap for you and your loved ones. Keep your spiritual eyes and ears open, to see and hear what Holy Spirit quickens to you. He may bring specific situations to mind. If this happens, bring those specifics to God in prayer. Imagine standing in front of the cross. The price has been paid. And this is your opportunity to lay those burdens down, repent and ask for forgiveness, knowing that when we confess our sins, He is faithful and just to forgive.

Below is an example of a prayer for you to pray out aloud in the company of your witnesses.

Sample Prayer:

> Holy Spirit, I welcome you. I acknowledge Your presence. Jesus, thank You that you intercede on my behalf, and because of You, I now have access to my King and Father.
>
> Papa God, thank You that I can come before You in the Name of Jesus, and personally petition You on behalf of my bloodline. Thank You that Your promises are clear, that whatever I bind on earth will be bound in heaven, and whatever I loose on earth will be loosed in heaven.
>
> Thank You that when two of us agree about anything we ask for, it *will* be done by You, our Lord and King.
>
> Lord, by the power and anointing of Holy Spirit, I ask You now to forgive every member of my bloodline, from my ancestors to the youngest living, who may have opened a door to the demonic realm.
>
> I repent on behalf of my bloodline, and I ask You Lord to forgive us.

Thank You for your promise that if we confess our sins, You are faithful and just to forgive us of our sins, and to cleanse us from all unrighteous.

Lord God, I stand on Your promises.

Thank You that You are washing my bloodline clean, through the blood of Jesus that was poured out on Calvary. Thank You, that whom the Son sets free, is free indeed, and I give You all the glory and all the honour, for healing and restoring my bloodline.

I commit to living the rest of my life in pursuit of you. I will teach and train the generations after me in your ways. I love You Lord, and I give You praise. In Jesus Name, Amen.

If you prayed that prayer on behalf of you and your bloodline, know that your God in Heaven hears you. 1 John 1:7 NKJV says, 'But if we walk in the light as He is in the light, we have fellowship with one another, and the blood of Jesus Christ His Son cleanses us from all sin.'

Take a moment to exhale. It is done.

2. Mental Pillar

Examples of seeds sown by the doors we open to our mind include anxiety, depression, suicidal thoughts, guilt, shame, condemnation. Other examples include believing anything that counters the truth of what God says about you. Lies that you are not good enough, that you don't have what it takes. Lies that you will forever battle with patterns of the past.

There's a saying that, 'the eyes are a gateway to the soul'. Maybe there are doors that you've opened yourself up to visually, that have had a knock-on-effect on your thought processes. For example: pornography, attending strip-clubs and opening one's-self up to prostitution, or sleeping around. Walking through these doors leaves footprints on the mind that can only be healed and restored through the blood of Jesus.

Some of the lies seeded in your mind may be from when you were young, and sadly by the very people whom you loved and trusted. Some of these doors were opened unknowingly, yet the lies have taken root within your heart, and have formed the basis of your beliefs, feelings, and in turn, your words and actions.

Take a moment to close your eyes and pray in the Spirit. Ask Holy Spirit to quicken your heart. Then wait. As Holy Spirit speaks, write down what He reveals to you, so that you can bring it all before the cross. He may reveal matters relating to you personally, or to do with someone within your family, who Holy Spirit highlights to you, in order for you to bridge the gap on their behalf. You don't have to labour over this. Holy Spirit will make very clear if there's anything specific that needs to be addressed.

Below is an example of a prayer for you to pray out aloud in the company of witnesses.

Sample Prayer:

> Holy Spirit, thank You for Your presence. Thank You that You are my helper, my advocate and friend. I acknowledge You, and I ask that You bring fresh revelation concerning my thoughts right now. If there is someone within my bloodline who needs me to bridge the gap, I choose to stand in the gap on their behalf also. As the Word says in Psalm 19:14 NKJV, 'Let the words of my mouth and the meditation of my heart be acceptable in Your sight, O Lord, my strength and my Redeemer.' That is my prayer today.

Jesus, thank You that You intercede on my behalf to the Father. Lord God, I acknowledge You as my Lord and King. I petition You, and I repent for every thought that has displeased and dishonoured You. I ask that You purify and cleanse my mind and my heart from the inside out. Make me pure like snow. I repent for every door opened that has impacted my thought processes and my beliefs. I cut off everything that is not in alignment with You. I accept and submit to the chastening of Holy Spirit. I accept and submit to His warnings, and I tune my ears to listen, and I open my eyes to see what the Spirit of God is saying.

I am deciding from this moment on, that I will *recognise* the voice of the enemy. I will *reject* his lies, and I will *replace* those lies with the truth of Your Word. I choose to stand on Romans 12:2 NKJV, 'And do not be conformed to this world, but be transformed by the renewing of your mind, that you may prove what is that good and acceptable and perfect will of God.'

Heavenly Father, I bridge the gap on behalf of my bloodline, to the thousandth generation. I choose blessings on their behalf. I choose life, and I ask for Your supernatural intervention, to heal and restore the minds of my family line. I give You all the glory and all the honour. In Jesus Name I pray, Amen.

Pause. Exhale. It is done.

3. Emotional Pillar

Examples of seeds sown by the doors we may have opened to our emotions can include imposter syndrome, (where you don't feel worthy of the position you carry), self-loathing, anger which leads to doing things we later regret, jealousy, hopelessness, stress, worry, sadness, disappointment, fear, panic, doubt, confusion. All of these examples impact our emotions and derail us from the plans and purposes of God. We live in a society that elevates emotions above being led by the Spirit of God. Let us not be like the world. Let us bring our emotions into alignment with what God is saying. He says you are blood bought. You are a child of the King, and you have access to the resources of Heaven to live out the life that God has put you on this earth for. A life of impact and generational change. A life that is to be lived in alignment and partnership with who God says you are.

When your emotions are in alignment with the Spirit of God, they will follow the fruit of His Spirit. For example: When you are wrapped in His love, your emotions will experience a profound sense of warmth, connection, selfless devotion. You will have feelings of security, belonging and a desire to uplift others.

When you experience His joy, there's a deep, abiding gladness that isn't dependent on the circumstances around you. Instead, when you find yourself in the eye of the storm, you will be filled with strength because you are appropriating the joy of His Spirit.

When you are filled with His peace, your emotions will experience a calming assurance and steadiness, like an anchor in the storm. The fruit of His peace fosters feelings of rest, trust and unshakable confidence in our God.

Why not spend some time in prayer right now. Ask Holy Spirit to highlight any doors that have been opened in your life that have negatively impacted your emotions. Doors that have caused emotional instability that need to be brought before the Lord and closed.

Below is an example of a prayer for you to pray out aloud in the company of witnesses.

Sample Prayer:

> Spirit of God, I welcome You. I acknowledge Your presence. Thank You for who You are in my life. I want to take a moment right now to hear from You. What doors have I opened and allowed to mould and shape my emotions? What am I feeding my emotions with, that does not align with who I am in You?

> Jesus, I thank You that Your cleansing blood was poured out so that I would not be trapped in imposter syndrome, self-loathing, anger, jealousy, hopelessness, stress, worry, sadness, disappointment, fear, panic, doubt, confusion. You came to cleanse me from everything that kills, steals and destroys, and I'm sorry for the times I have allowed the voice of this world to drown out what You did for me on Calvary.

> Father God, I come before You right now as Your child, and I ask You to cleanse my emotions. Purify me from the inside out. I choose to come into alignment with what You say about me. I ask that through the power of Your Spirit, You awaken me, and remove the calluses from my eyes, so I can identify the different emotions I experience in any given day, that are not in alignment with You. I choose right now to submit my emotions under Your authority.

I choose to stand against emotions led by my flesh, and I clothe myself in a garment of praise, to lift off the spirit of heaviness as You promise in Isaiah 61:3 NKJV, 'To console those who mourn in Zion, To give them beauty for ashes, The oil of joy for mourning, The garment of praise for the spirit of heaviness; That they may be called trees of righteousness, The planting of the Lord, that He may be glorified.'

Thank You Father that You are changing me from the inside out.

I bring every emotion within my bloodline into submission of You. We will no longer be led by the things of the flesh, but instead I choose on behalf of my family, lives of blessings and not cursings to the thousandth generation as You promise. I grab a hold of Your promises Oh God, and I receive them with thankfulness of heart. In Jesus Name, Amen.

4. Physical Pillar

The choices we make sow seeds for life and blessing, or for death and cursing. There is no in-between. When we open certain doors, we give the enemy the right to kill, steal and destroy. (John 10:10).

Some of those doors opened in the physical can lead to addictions such as gambling, smoking, drugs, alcohol, pornography, masturbation, or sex outside of God's design. Other doors can lead to destructive actions like abuse, adultery, murder, rape, domestic violence, and all result from us giving our body, legal right to such behaviours. Each of these choices of action leads to deeper cycles of pain and brokenness, pulling us further away from the life God intends for us. The fruit we bear in our lives, be it good or bad, is a direct result of the seeds we sow. The question is, what kind of harvest are we producing? What fruit are we bearing?

Take a moment to consider your harvest. What fruit is *your* life bearing, and what is the ripple effect of your fruit on the lives of those around you?

Galatians 5:19-25 NKJV is clear. 'Now the works of the flesh are evident, which are: adultery, fornication, uncleanness, lewdness, idolatry, sorcery, hatred, contentions, jealousies, outburst of wrath, selfish ambitions, dissensions, heresies, envy, murders, drunkenness, revelries and the lie; of which I tell you beforehand, just as I told you in time past, that those who practice such things will not inherit the kingdom of God.

But the fruit of the Spirit is love, joy, peace, longsuffering, kindness, goodness, faithfulness, gentleness, self-control. Against such there is no law. And those who are Christ's have crucified the flesh with its passions and desires. If we live in the Spirit, let us walk in the Spirit.'

Just as the fruit of the flesh is evident to all, so is, and so will be, the fruit of the Spirit in your life. If some of the fruit you are bearing is not honouring or pleasing before the Lord and is potentially sabotaging you living in the fulness of who God has created you to be, then maybe now is the time to bring these matters before the Lord and close some doors.

Below is an example of a prayer for you to pray out aloud in the company of witnesses. Like I have said before, if you don't have someone who can physically be present with you, ask Holy Spirit to be your witness.

Sample Prayer:

> Holy Spirit, thank You for Your presence. Thank You that you are my advocate, my guide, and my friend. Thank You that You are revealing to me the areas within my life that

need to come into alignment, in order for me to step into the fullness of who God has created me to be. I ask that You fill me afresh right now. Holy Spirit, have Your way.

Jesus, thank You that You intercede on my behalf to Abba Father. I come before You with humility of spirit, and I repent of everything that I have done that has saddened Your heart. It is my sole desire to please You, and to live a life that honours and represents Your Name well.

Papa God, I love You. I am so thankful for Your Son, who has granted me access to You. I do not take lightly the fact that I can come boldly into Your presence, and deal with the matters that have been holding me back.

I come before You in total and utter surrender. I'm sorry for the doors that I have opened in my life, that have led me down a path of behaviours that do not please You. Please forgive me. Wash me clean through the cleansing blood of Your Son, Jesus, and purify me from all unrighteousness. (As Holy Spirit points out specific behaviours, address them before your King now. For example: Lord, I close the door on pornography. I make a choice decision that I will not feed my flesh, but instead, I will saturate myself with Your Spirit. I recognise that this is not of You. I reject it, and I replace it with time spent in Your presence. Lord, I acknowledge that I cannot do this without You. Empower me through Your Spirit, to be able to resist the temptations of this world, so that my life reflects Your glory.)

Lord, I come before You on behalf of my bloodline. I repent on behalf of my ancestors who have gone before me. I close the doors that they opened, that have negatively impacted our generations. I stand in the gap for my bloodline to the thousandth generation, and I appropriate Your promises, for they are yes and AMEN.

In Jesus Name I pray, Amen.

Now give thanks to the Lord, for He is good. His mercies endure forever. Exhale. It is done.

5. Relational Pillar

Examples of seeds sown by the doors we open in this pillar may include entering into toxic or abusive relationships, being unable to maintain healthy relationships, self-sabotage, gender dysphoria, eating disorders, promiscuity, as well as isolating oneself from others. Wherever there is lack within our relationships, we can come before the Lord, acknowledge the gaps, and ask Him to fill us with supernatural foresight to see where the enemy has had legal right to kills, steal and destroy. We can ask for supernatural wisdom to navigate the changes that need to be made, which He promises in James 1:5 NKJV, 'If any of you lacks wisdom, let him ask of God, who gives to all liberally and without reproach, and it will be given to him.' But as the passage continues, we must approach our God in faith, knowing that He is a God of His word. James 1:6 NKJV says, 'But let him ask in faith, with no doubting, for he who doubts is like a wave of the sea driven and tossed by the wind.' Let us not wade in the pool of flaky Christianity. We need to know who we are, whose we are, and who's authority we carry, so that we can be warriors of the Most High God, who bridge the gap for ourselves and our people.

Take a moment to consider the relationships you have with your loved ones. How healthy are these relationships, both for you, and for them? Are you someone who brings out the best in your family, friends and colleagues? Or are you the cause of provocation and exasperation? Are some relationships so toxic, that you actually need to walk away?

Ask Holy Spirit to bring to mind any relationships that need to be addressed. You may see a person's face or have a specific scenario flash before you. Turn on your spiritual senses so that you can see and hear what the Spirit of God is saying.

When you're ready, below is an example of a prayer for you to pray out aloud in the company of witnesses.

Sample Prayer:

> Spirit of God, thank You that I can call on You to discuss anything. Nothing is hidden from You, and I don't need to be ashamed of addressing openly and honestly, the matters that I struggle with. It is in my confession that these issues are brought to light, with You Holy Spirit as my witness, so that through the power and blood of Jesus, I can be set free.
>
> Jesus, I acknowledge You as my Lord and Saviour. There is none like You. And right now, I bring my relationships before You. (Name them, one by one. Don't hold back). I lift the weight of these relationships off my shoulders, and I place them at the foot of the empty cross. You came that I may have life in abundance, and I take back the territory that the enemy has stolen in my relationships, right now. I

close the door on any and every relationship that is not of You. Highlight those relationships to me through the power of Your Spirit. I declare that the enemy no longer has a foothold in my relationships from this point on. Thank You for Your promise that whom You set free, IS free. I receive that promise in Your Holy Name. (See John 8:36)

Father God, I ask that You bestow upon me Your wisdom from heaven, to discern right from wrong, truth from lies. Empower me through Your Spirit to uplift, edify, and encourage every single person in my world. May I be a source of life to them. Help me to filter out the noise. I tune my ears to You, and I choose to live in accordance with the truth of Your Word. May my life reflect You well, to everyone whom I have the privilege of doing life with.

And Lord, I'm sorry on behalf of myself and my bloodline, for all unhealthy doors opened relationally. I ask for Your forgiveness, and I ask that You cover my bloodline's relationships to the thousandth generation. I bridge the gap, and I stand on Your promises. In Jesus Name, Amen.

Take a moment to give thanks to God for what He has done and is yet to do.

6. Financial Pillar

Matthew 6:21 NIV says, 'For where your treasure is, there your heart will be also.'

Examples of financial seeds sown by the doors we open, that ultimately lead to destruction - include the funding of addictions such as gambling, drugs, alcohol, pornography or prostitution, to name a few. The ripple effect doesn't just impact one's bank account, but one's life as a whole. Every single pillar in the human life is affected.

Is it time for a financial audit? Is it time to pull up those bank statements, and assess exactly where your money is going?

The fact is, if you don't look after your money, the world will take every penny, and suck you dry in the process. So where does your heart lie? Pull up those bank statements and you'll find out.

Highlight the transactions that Holy Spirit quickens to you. Maybe there are some places that you've been visiting that you shouldn't be. Maybe there's subscriptions on the go, that are feeding those fleshly habits that are subtly sabotaging your physical, mental, emotional, spiritual, relational and financial wellbeing.

This exercise isn't to stir up guilt or shame. No. If you feel this way, shake it off – it's a lie from the enemy, designed to keep you trapped, and keep what's hidden in the dark. It's only as we surrender and submit these matters before our God, that we allow Him access to do what only He can do. He breathes new life, new revelation, healing and restoration from the inside out.

When you're ready, bring what you discover from your financial audit to the table, and let's do business with our God, because as He says in 1 John 1:9 NIV, 'If we confess our sins, He is faithful and just and will forgive us our sins and purify us from all unrighteousness.'

Below is an example of a prayer for you to pray out aloud in the company of witnesses.

Sample Prayer:

> Holy Spirit, I welcome You. Thank You for Your presence. Thank You for strengthening me and getting me to this

place of surrender. I acknowledge your transformative power at work in me, and I ask for your help right now.

Jesus, I thank You that Your blood is more powerful than any addiction. Thank You that I get to partner with You, and as I surrender and submit to the change process in my life, I hold the authority to close doors in Your Name, and to open new doors to a life of healing, restoration, revival, renewal, strength, might, wisdom beyond my years, and the ability to bear good fruit.

Father God, I humbly bring my finances before You. Lord I am sorry for (list whatever you have found that you know in your heart does not bring glory to your precious Father) …

I repent for subscribing to… I no longer accept this as my portion. I can see how the enemy has used this to short-circuit what You have in store for me, and so I close that door in the spirit realm right now.

Thank You Lord, that You promise in Your Word in Matthew 18:18 NIV, 'Assuredly, I say to you, whatever you bind on earth will be bound in heaven, and whatever you loose on earth will be loosed in heaven.' Father God, thank You that I am loosed from the bondage of sin. I am blood bought, I am Your child, and I thank You that through the power of Your Spirit, my physical, mental, emotional, spiritual, relational and financial pillars are coming into alignment with You.

But I thank You, even more so, that I can bridge the gap on behalf of my whole, entire bloodline. And so, Lord, I do this right now. I say sorry, and I ask for forgiveness for every door opened and effected in the finances of my ancestors. I break those sins and curses off my bloodline, and I pray healing, restoration, and prosperity over my bloodline to the thousandth generation, as You promise. I come against the spirit of poverty. I surrender and submit all of my finances to You. You are my Lord and King. You alone are my Master. Money is there to serve and help facilitate the expansion of Your Kingdom, and I choose to do my part. Hold me to account. Quicken me by Your Spirit, so that I honour you with the resources you entrust into my hand. I stand on Your promises, and I step out in obedience, and oh God, I give You praise. In Jesus Name, Amen.

IN CLOSING

Before I bring this book to a close, I must share with you that Björn returned home after six months in rehab – completely transformed.

We will be forever grateful to the men and women who played an active role in his recovery. To our family and friends who stood by us, prayed on the sidelines, and believed for breakthrough on our behalf - Sandro and I love and honour you.

As I pen these final words, I find myself sitting in my hotel room in Adelaide, on the tenth-year anniversary of Björn's stem cell transplant, in awe of all that Papa God has done. It also happens to be the beginning of Lent – the forty-day journey leading up to Easter, when we celebrate the outpouring of Jesus' blood for the cleansing and freedom of all sin and curses.

Björn has several medical appointments lined up over the next couple of days and will, of course be seeing Dr Nick, a man who has not only walked this road as Björn's Neurologist, but as a dear friend.

Bringing this book to a close feels particularly poignant as memories from the last ten years – let alone a lifetime – come flooding back. Björn's involvement, along with that of other young men who participated in the clinical trial, has been instrumental in providing the evidence that led to this treatment's FDA (Food & Drug Administration, USA) approval. This breakthrough now offers hope to children around the world who are battling the same hereditary illness.

And now a personal message to you my precious reader. I believe that through the reading of this book you have become more aware of the spiritual forces at play – the unseen battle over your life. You now understand how crucial it is to filter the thoughts that penetrate your mind, and to be selective as to what you allow to take root in your heart.

I believe that the eyes of your understanding have been opened, and you are walking away equipped – not only with the knowledge of how to identify and break generational sins and curses off your own life but to also change the trajectory of future generations through the power and authority of Jesus that flows in and through you.

Too many Christians are living a life that is short-changed because they don't fully grasp who they are, or the authority they carry in Christ. It is my prayer that as this book finds itself within homes around the world – and now, in your very own hands - a fresh revelation of your identity and authority in Jesus will ignite within you, like the flicking of a switch.

It has been my honour to recount and articulate my personal journey of faith, redemption, love and healing. I pray that this book has blessed and equipped you in ways you didn't expect. But remember, it's not enough to have head knowledge. Now is the time for applied knowledge. So, step out. Walk in your God-given identity and authority. Com before Him. Break the generational bondage that has held your family captive. And may you be the vessel God uses to rewrite your family's future.

As I bring this book to a close, I leave you with one final challenge:

Who in your world needs to read this book? Maybe you have a friend battling depression, anxiety, or suicidal thoughts. Or perhaps a loved one whose grandmother died of cancer, whose mother died of cancer – who now they live in fear that they, too, will die of cancer.

May I encourage you to sow a seed of generosity? Invest in the lives of those you love. Get a few extra copies of this book, write a personal message in each, sharing how it has impacted you, and then gift it to them. Let's stand in faith and watch how Papa God uses the stories and tools etched within these pages to set other families free.

ACKNOWLEDGEMENTS

Firstly, I want to acknowledge and give thanks to my Papa God for little Ashok. If it wasn't for his short life, I may never have stepped into the wardrobe.

Little Ashok, I love you bro. When we meet again in glory, you can show me the fields of yellow.

My Babe, my hubby, my best friend, Sandro. You have supported me from day dot. While we had to let go of our dream home all those years ago, look at what our Papa God has opened up before us. This is just the beginning Babe. I love you.

Ramon, your name means *wise protection*, and that is exactly who you have been to our family. In our darkest moments, when we had no one else, you stepped in with wisdom beyond your years. While I wasn't laughing then, I can't help but giggle at the memory of us raiding your brother's room together. The action steps you demanded - at times when we couldn't see the wood from the trees – quite literally saved us. We are endlessly grateful for you and so incredibly proud of the man you have become.

Björn, there are no words to describe how proud we are to be your earthly mama and papa. You've been through so much, yet you are still standing. We are so thankful for your life, your resilience and tenacity.

Thank you for allowing me to share my perspective. People around the world are being impacted by our stories and we all can't wait to read *your* version one day.

Mom and Dad, thank you for allowing God to heal your hearts. If it wasn't for your surrender and submission to the process, you wouldn't have heard the cries of your second-born, to take the brave step of having more children. Thank you for allowing your lives to be a walking, talking testimony to the healing power of God. I love you more than you will ever know.

Sam, I love you bro. You are a gift to my heart, and I give thanks to God for your life every single day. You've helped me heal.

Hannah, my precious sis. I didn't want Sam to be alone like I was, and even though you raided my makeup as a little girl and irritated me to no end, you have become one of the most incredible women I know. I love you.

To Dr Apaks Dede and Dawuta Dede—our dear, dear friends.

Apaks, there are no words vast enough to encapsulate the depth of our gratitude. You did more than provide medical care—you saved our son's life. Your unwavering dedication, your expertise, and your compassion are nothing short of extraordinary. The impact of your work ripples far beyond what the eye can see, shaping not just the lives of those you heal but also the hearts of those who witness your selfless service. Your well-deserved recognition as Specialist (Non-GP) of the Year in the Western Australia Rural Health Excellence Awards is a testament to your outstanding dedication and impact. The world needs more paediatricians like you.

Dawuta, your warmth, your kindness, and the grace with which you walk this journey alongside Apaks inspires us deeply. Your friendship has become a cherished gift, a steady presence that we hold close to our hearts.

We are forever grateful for you both, not just for what you have done, but for who you are.

Dr Nicholas Smith, Dr Shanti Balasubramaniam, Dr Satiro De Oliveira, Dr Theodore B Moore, Dayna, Louise, and every dedicated member of the team who stood alongside us throughout Björn's medical journey - Your dedication and sacrifice over the years have not only blessed our family but countless others who have walked through your doors. Your service is more than a profession – it is a calling, and we are eternally grateful for the care, wisdom, and compassion you have poured into our journey.

Auntie Bev, I think Uncle Kev and little Ashok are singing that song together. Here's to the day when we will all join the chorus.

Heidi, Patricia & Susan, you were there for me when I was right in the thick of the trenches. I will be forever grateful for your friendship because you literally carried the load when I didn't have the strength to lift any longer.

Christine & Richard, in the short time we've known you, you've wholeheartedly embraced our ministry, becoming cherished friends along the way. We thank the Lord for you and deeply treasure and honour you. Buckle up—this journey is just beginning!

To our loved ones in Australia, the United Kingdom, USA, Asia, Africa and all around the world, you know who you are. You hold a special place in our hearts.

180TC, your unwavering support – physically, mentally, emotionally, spiritually, relationally and financially – was nothing short of lifesaving. You stood in the gap and changed the trajectory of our son's life. There are no words to fully express our gratitude. We don't just thank you on behalf of our family, but on behalf of every family whose lives you continue to transform.

Holy Spirit, I've called on You so much throughout the living out and writing of this book. Thank You for being my ever-present help. I love and honour You.

Jesus, I wouldn't be here if it wasn't for You. Thank You for the wardrobe moments. I will continue to step in, all the days of my life.

Papa God, thank You for loving me. Thank You for using me, despite me. May this book bring glory and honour to Your Name.

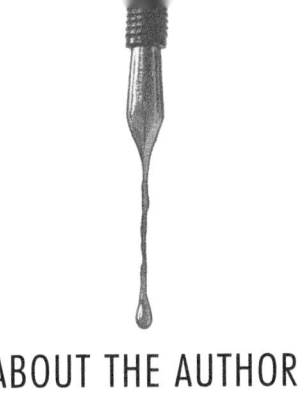

ABOUT THE AUTHOR

Nalini Tranquim is a transformational coach, prophetic voice, and storyteller whose work challenges, inspires, and equips people to step into their God-given identity. As a musician, author, and podcast host, she weaves together raw authenticity, deep spiritual insight, and a passion for truth to create powerful spaces for healing and breakthrough.

Based in Melbourne, Australia, Nalini's journey has been one of resilience—rising from personal trials to become a chain-breaker and revivalist, dedicated to seeing lives transformed. Her influence spans across multiple platforms, from Under the Rug, a podcast that uncovers the unspoken battles we face, to The Wardrobe, a deeply personal album that calls listeners into intimacy with God. Her work extends beyond music and media into coaching programs, speaking engagements, and mentorship, equipping individuals—especially the next generation—to step into their authority with boldness and clarity.

Through her storytelling, whether in song, books, or public speaking engagements, Nalini doesn't just share a message—she invites her audience into a movement of authenticity, healing, and purpose.

Face As Flint Publishing, PO Box 8009,
Kooyong, 3144, Victoria, Australia

www.ingramcontent.com/pod-product-compliance
Lightning Source LLC
Chambersburg PA
CBHW032113090426
42743CB00007B/336